Beautiful

Thinking

Dulcinea
Norton-Morris

To my lovely father Peter, with whom I shared a love of literature and writing, I only wish you could have read this book. To Momo, my best friend, most analytical critic and biggest fan. To Bobo, my inspirational philosopher. Finally, to my lovely Danny, who puts up with me tapping away on my laptop late into the night and never once complains. You are all the kindest and most loving people I have ever known. Thank you.

Love Dulcie

x

Inspired by the book *Thinking Moves A-Z* by Roger Sutcliffe

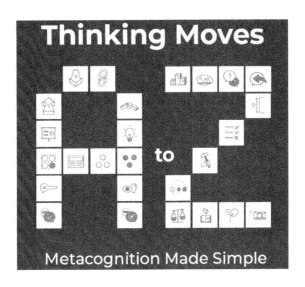

Thinking Moves A-Z, Roger Sutcliffe, Jason Buckley, and Tom Bigglestone

https://www.thephilosophyman.com/product/thinking-moves-a-z

To access all the latest Thinking Moves opportunities, training, and resources, go to:

www.dialogueworks.co.uk/thinking-moves

Co-published by:

DIALOGUE WORKS

DialogueWorks Ltd

59 Falkland Road, London, NW52XB, UK

Email: bobhouse@dialogueworks.co.uk

Web: www.dialogueworks.co.uk

Magical Mess of the EYFS

Twitter: @DulcineaEYFS

Web: https://magicalmess.weebly.com

Facebook: @MagicalEYFS

Illustrations by Dulcinea Norton-Morris. Thinking Moves images courtesy of DialogueWorks.Public domain illustrations from freevintageillustrations.comn. Additional images by Halfppoint, Odua, Monkeybusiness, Seventyfourimages, nenetus, Satura_, leungchopin, Rawpixel, Prostock-studio, and Dragonimages at Photodune.net

Acknowledgements

I would like to say a huge thanks to Roger Sutcliffe, Bob House and Nick Chandley, who have inspired and supported me and always give me new fuel for thought. Without them, this book would never have existed. Each in their separate ways, they serve as a constant inspiration to me, and I can only hope to have a portion of their metacognitive skills and intelligence one day.

Thank you to my early readers, Fufy and Ann-Marie. Fufy Demissie is the most amazing Senior Lecturer, who is inspiring new generations of Early Years teachers every day as she looks to the future of using philosophical teaching approaches in Early Years education. Ann-Marie McNicholas is a specialist teacher and author who I admire so very much.

Thank you to all of the philosophers at large who have contributed case studies. To Sorcha, who has a deep understanding of the benefits of Thinking Moves with young children and inspires and supports other practitioners as they begin to explore Thinking Moves. To Amanda, who is taking Thinking Moves to the next level in nursery teaching and to support all children no matter what their barriers. To Gina, the queen of philosophy in the outdoors and nature, whose love of Philosophy for Children got me hooked in the first place. To Ella, who is an author, illustrator and thinker of the future. Finally, to Jorge, who showed me how much Thinking Moves can be adapted to be translatable in all languages and the true power it has in creating a culture of equality.

A huge thank you to my friends who have supported and encouraged me over the past ten years of writing, had endless Early Years chats with me, and have advised on everything from book cover design to "shut up, get off WhatsApp and go to sleep now". I don't want to miss anyone off my list, but you know who you are.

Finally, a thank you to my three boys and to the children I have taught over the years for being my child development research and Thinking Moves Guinea pigs without even knowing it.

Table of Contents

Thinking Moves A-Z

DIALOGUE WORKS

	THINKING MOVES	EARLY YEARS SYNONYMS
A	AHEAD	LOOK FORWARD
B	BACK	LOOK BACK
C	CONNECT	SAY WHAT'S THE SAME
D	DIVIDE	SAY WHAT'S DIFFERENT
E	EXPLAIN	SAY WHAT HAPPENED
F	FORMULATE	HAVE AN IDEA / PUT INTO WORDS
G	GROUP	PUT INTO GROUPS
H	HEADLINE	SAY IN A FEW WORDS
I	INFER	TELL FROM
J	JUSTIFY	SAY WHY
K	KEYWORD	PICK THE IMPORTANT WORD
L	LOOK / LISTEN	USE YOUR SENSES
M	MAINTAIN	SAY WHAT YOU THINK
N	NEGATE	SAY NO
O	ORDER	PUT IN ORDER
P	PICTURE	SEE IN YOUR MIND
Q	QUESTION	ASK
R	RESPOND	SAY SOMETHING ABOUT
S	SIZE	SAY HOW BIG
T	TEST	MAKE SURE
U	USE	TRY OUT
V	VARY	TRY A DIFFERENT WAY
W	WEIGH UP	CHOOSE
X	eXEMPLIFY	GIVE AN EXAMPLE
Y	YIELD	CHANGE YOUR MIND
Z	ZOOM	LOOK CLOSELY

Foreword by Roger Sutcliffe

When I formulated the idea of dividing human thought processes into fundamental 'moves', and then squeezing them into alphabetical order, I did not anticipate that it would take nearly ten years to get the scheme ready for publication. Looking back, I had no idea of the size of the task I had set myself. But, with help and encouragement from colleagues, the project came to fruition in 2019. We waited anxiously to see if the idea would be taken up.

To be honest, we were confident that it would go down well in primary schools – and early tests proved it so – and we now have growing confidence of take up in secondary schools and even businesses. What none of us quite pictured, though, was that Early Years teachers would be amongst the first to put it to good use. How foolish of us!

Early Years teachers in the UK are renowned for looking and finding new ways of stimulating young minds, and varying those ways to suit their unique classes. Dulcinea Norton-Morris stands out, even among such a talented group, for her creativity – I might even say, genius. Within a very short while she had not only introduced the Thinking Moves to her very young children; she had also created games and activities that enabled them to become integral to her teaching and their learning.

So much – so good! But now she has taken a yet further step and collated all that practice, and some wonderful thinking about that practice, into what amounts to a handbook for developing 'beautiful' thinking in beautiful babies, toddlers and pre-schoolers. It is a handbook equally helpful to parents as to teachers, and Dulcie's experience and expertise in relating to people of such tender years jumps out from each page. Every new parent will connect with her anecdotes and observations, and will appreciate her explanations and examples, not only of children's behaviour but also of their capacities.

She has headlined and ordered the chapters in a clear way to enable adults caring for children of different ages or special circumstances to find what they are looking for easily. I would particularly recommend Chapter 14, even though, or even because, it is about children older than those who will most immediately benefit from the book. It is in this chapter that Dulcie's philosophy of teaching-and-learning expresses itself most powerfully – a philosophy that shows deep purpose and is devoted to best practice. For sure, P4C (Philosophy for Children) has influenced both this purpose and this practice. But this is only because she is quite clearly the sort of person – not just the sort of teacher – you would want by your side as you equip your own child with her / his own philosophy of life. Thank goodness for such teachers, and for such a vision of education!

Roger Sutcliffe, August 2020

PART 1

THINKING MOVES FROM BIRTH TO FIVE

Introduction

"A white rabbit is pulled out of a top hat. Because it is an extremely large rabbit, the trick takes many billions of years. All mortals are born at the very tip of the rabbit's fine hairs. where they are in a position to wonder at the impossibility of the trick. But as they grow older they work themselves even deeper into the fur. And there they stay. They become so comfortable they never risk crawling back up the fragile hairs again. Only philosophers embark on this perilous expedition to the outermost reaches of language and existence."

(Jostein Gaardner, Sophie's World *(Phoenix, 1995)*

For those of us who choose to live in the world of Early Years, either as parents or practitioners, we are witnessing the most exciting time of human life when there is still a universe of possibilities open to our mini philosophers.

Philosophers may once have been seen as old and wise, but nowadays, our greatest philosophers are far younger. One of the favourite methods of Socrates was to keep asking,' why?'. I think that he may have stolen this method from a three-year-old.

At the start of each school year, my class is made up entirely of three-year-olds. They are still babies in most people's eyes. Very few understand 'why' and 'how' questions when posed by other people, though they ask 'why?' themselves continually and to distraction. Very few even understand what a question is.

Ask a class of three and four-year-olds if they have a question they would like to ask, and you will be met with a barrage of information instead, such as, "I'm getting a Peppa Pig bike for Christmas" or "I like pizza." So, when first dipping my toe into Philosophy for Children, I was, understandably, dubious. I was wrong. It turns out that the under-fives are the perfect philosophers, and they have been doing it their entire lives!

Children are born without preconceptions and with no knowledge of the 'truth' or 'facts.' From the minute we sing them a nursery rhyme, read a book, or pop on the TV, they are presented with talking animals, flying superheroes, and wizards with magic wands.

We tell them little white lies about the Tooth Fairy and Santa. Terry Pratchett suggests in his book, *The Hogfather* (Terry Pratchett, [Victor Gollancz] 1996), that these fantasy-based lies create an essential way of thinking in children. It is a form of thinking in which they can learn to suspend disbelief and so later learn about and accept invisible concepts such as justice, love, and hope. In a more scientific vein, this helps a child to accept later equally intangible concepts (to a child's eye at any rate) such as photosynthesis and atoms.

After a couple of years of doing Philosophy for Children with my class, I became comfortable enough to begin to experiment, and it was then that I discovered Roger Sutcliffe's *Thinking Moves*[1]. This book and approach break metacognition skills down into a handy A-Z. As I explored it further, I realised that Thinking Moves A-Z provided me with a holistic approach that tied philosophy and the wonder of childhood together beautifully. It was also accessible to my children with communication difficulties as each move comes with a sign language action. It was instantly understandable to me as it was made up of twenty-six words that I already knew and were easy to use, yet Thinking Moves continues to amaze me every day as I learn more about it. The more you work with each move, the more you realise how much depth, flexibility and relevance each one offers.

I will mention different Thinking Moves throughout this book, and you will find both references to them in the text (which show how instinctive the moves are) and some more specific ideas and activities. A lot of the suggestions will be ones that you can build into your everyday holistic practice or interactions with children with minimal effort needed. Thinking Moves is a complete metacognition approach to interacting with young children, but do not let the word 'metacognition' trick you into thinking you need a philosophy degree to understand it. It just means thinking about thinking.

I will also show you my QUEST model, which makes planning your activities quick and easy, whether just planning a quick five-minute game or challenging yourself with a more formal Philosophy for Children (P4C) session. If you do not know much about Philosophy for Children, don't worry. At the back of the book, you will find details of many organisations and websites for you to look into P4C further and information about formal Thinking Moves training if that is something you would like to pursue.

You don't need to be doing P4C at all to use this approach as, although Thinking Moves sits well with Philosophy for Children, it is a metacognition approach which can be used entirely on its own as part of your usual Early Years practice.

At some points in this book, I will refer to children as if they are the ones you are caring for professionally. At other points, I will refer to them as if they were your own child. This is because a Thinking Moves approach can be used by practitioners and parents alike. I use them explicitly and implicitly in my classroom, and I find myself using them stealthily at home too.

Thinking Moves have helped me to support my eldest son through GCSEs and choosing a college course, my middle son through his usual quandary (how to spend his birthday money), and I am using them more explicitly to try to increase the vocabulary and understanding of my summer-born baby of the class who is starting Reception Class just one week after his fourth birthday. We also use them as a fun framework for our bedtime chat, unknown to my four-year-old. In the appendices, you can see how I do this. It has now become a habit.

You will find the actual Thinking Moves A-Z with their Early Years Synonyms at the beginning of this book, courtesy of DialogueWorks (https://dialogueworks.co.uk/). I heartily recommend you visit the website yourself, where you will find a wealth of resources and ideas and the link to buy the original *Thinking Moves A-Z* book, which inspired me to write *Beautiful Thinking*.

Chapter 1 – Why Are Children Natural Philosophers?

There are no limits and no constraints in the way a child sees the world until they begin to grow up. That is when we adults either purposely or inadvertently teach them to live and think by the rules. Depressingly limiting rules of correct and incorrect thinking, of what is a sensible thought and what is a silly one. For a long time, children can grow up not worrying that something they say might be 'silly' or 'wrong,' and it is in this silly wrongness that they can explore the world and become the inventors and innovators of the future.

Philosophical teaching is a beautifully holistic way to approach early education. It grasps those precious moments of wonder that a child experiences every day and makes those moments count.

The National Geographic article 'Why We Lie: The Science Behind Our Deceptive Ways,'(1) discussed a study that claimed that children under the age of six lie less than any other age group. But these are the age group that gets lied to the most. Why? One reason for this is that we adults struggle to explain the big things. We lie about the things that we don't think our children are ready to know about and about the things we don't understand ourselves. Perhaps some of our lies would be better as philosophical introductions.

Picture this. A child has a very poorly grandparent. The child asks you, in class, "What will happen to Grandad when he dies?" What do you say? You don't know what the child's parents want you to say. Perhaps the child has not even asked them yet. You don't want to impose your own opinions or overstep the mark. You don't want to devalue their question or feelings by brushing the question off. So what do you do? You turn the child into a philosopher. After all, isn't that what we all are when it comes to trying to comprehend and cope with death? You instinctively say, "What do you think happens?" (QUESTION) and mentally curse yourself for taking the cowards way out. But in doing this, you allow the child to explore what their own thoughts are. When it comes down to it, can we really claim that we have any more idea of what happens to our soul after death than a three-year-old child does?

In this and many other areas, we are as equally knowledgeable as each other. That is the beauty of philosophy (in a P4C context, as opposed to an advanced level academic sense). Anyone can do it. We adults may be better at critical thinking and reasoning, but those three-year-olds really do beat us when it comes to creativity.

Being a parent or practitioner is tough. Children come in all different shapes and sizes – physically, emotionally, and academically – and there is no one size fits all approach to parenting them. Every child is different, and you don't need a fancy labelled parenting or teaching approach to deal with them (says the woman writing a book on a method with a label. Yes, I see the irony). It is an unfortunate truth of the world that not all children get a fair shot at life. It may be because of race, economic disadvantage, adverse childhood events, sexuality or gender issues (for them or their parents), the country or politics they are born into, or because of physical, emotional, or mental health disadvantages. There are so many things that make life very much, not a level playing field. For some children, this will impact them from birth (or before); for others, not until they get into later childhood. Unfortunately, a lot of problems will come from adults themselves, either as a result of systemic failings or personal prejudices. Teaching children philosophical skills teaches them how to deal with and try to overcome these barriers. It also gives us a fighting chance of creating new generations who are loving, tolerant, intelligent, and open-minded enough to tackle and fix all of the things about society and attitudes. I don't want to come over all evangelical and preachy about children being our future, but... they literally are!

My mum says that if only people would listen to the generations before them, then we would be able to learn from their mistakes and avoid making them. We would evolve generation by generation and have happy lives, but we don't because that isn't human nature at all. Once children reach a certain age, they begin to think that maybe their parents just don't understand the modern world at all, and their advice can't be valid. So, the best thing we can do, if we can't pass down that knowledge is to build creative and critical thinkers so that they can come up with the best solutions themselves.

Tiny humans are full-on! They are weird, crazy, wonderful, and desperate to take you along for the ride whether you like it or not. The unique thing about the under-fives is that they genuinely do believe in the things they conjure up in their imaginations. They have questions too. So, so many questions and they ask them ad infinitum. They are still in that period of their childhood when no question is silly. They play, they explore, imagine, and talk—a lot.

Birth to five is that magical, sparkly, dazzling, beautiful window of opportunity when children are like patches of well-tended soil, ready to receive their first philosophical seeds. The lucky ones are still living a beautiful life where all things are possible, but this stage can puff away like dandelion floss in an instant as soon as they begin to get older, and their thoughts become more rigid. This is the time to grab them by their chubby little hands and nurture their creative little brains.

In addition to being used as a holistic approach, Philosophy for Children and Thinking Moves can be used with any Early Years Curriculum to enhance different specific areas of learning. You will see some examples later in this book with both mine and Amanda Hubball's QUESTS. It is now being embraced in some Initial Teacher Training courses too.

In the UK, one university that is fully embracing a P4C approach in the Early Years is Sheffield Hallam University. Senior lecturer, Dr Fufy Demissie, is piloting a project with local nurseries which ties together the use of P4C with the Early Years curriculum. It starts with a literature input then being holistically integrated into other areas of learning, conversation, and child-led play in the following weeks.

References:

(1)Yudhijit Bhattacharjee *Why We Lie: The Science Behind Our Deceptive Ways* (National Geographic) 2017

Case Study: Teaching with Tales for Children (TWITCH)

By Dr Fufy Demissie

Teaching with Tales for Children (TWITCH) is a university and school project. It is supported by the SHINE Trust and designed to improve 3-5-year-olds language, questioning, and higher-order thinking skills using interactive story-based activities. At the same time, it aims to build practitioners' confidence and ability to ask open-ended questions that encourage children to think, justify, and reflect on their ideas. Through home learning packs, it also promotes parental involvement in the project.

The project builds on children's natural interest in stories and thinking games based on the Philosophy for Children (P4C) approach. Initially, practitioners are trained in the aims and principles of the P4C pedagogy. They learn to recognise the crucial concepts in stories and how these concept-based thinking games can deepen children's interest and engagement in stories. In Little Red Riding Hood, for example, 'danger,' 'strangers,' 'obedience' are some of the key concepts in the story. In the second part of the training, the practitioners experience these concept-based thinking games or themselves and begin to plan their own concept-based thinking activities.

The intervention is organised so that each story follows a three-week cycle.

In the first week, children are introduced to the story and the characters.

In the second seek, the practitioners offer a dilemma or choice-based question based on a concept in the story. Below are two examples:

The story: Goldilocks and the Three Bears

The thinking Game: 'Yes/No because...'

'Was Goldilocks a good girl? '

The story: Three Billy Goats Gruff

Thinking game: Agree/Disagree: 'the goats shouldn't eat other people's grasses, 'Little Billy Goats Gruff was not kind to his brother', etc.

'Who agrees?'

Once they have thought about the question, the children are invited to commit to a position (e.g. agree or disagree), justify their choice, and reflect on theirs and their friends' choices. The P4C methodology gives practitioners useful ways to encourage the children to reflect, such as 'Why do you think that?', 'What would happen if'?', 'What does 'xxx' mean?'. It also reminds them about the importance of genuine listening, adopting a curious attitude, and building on what the children say rather than impose their views and over-direct the discussion.

The third week is an opportunity to extend and embed the story through activities in small world play, cooking, re-writing a shared story, role play, and creative and explorative activities.

So far, the feedback suggests that both practitioners and children are enjoying the activity. According to one of the practitioners: It has been wonderful to see children's knowledge and language expand so much when given the time and space to explore and interpret stories in their own way.'.

The pilot phase will be followed by a roll out to a further five settings. The children's language and thinking will be evaluated using the Tower Hamlets language structure (focussing on the language for argumentation) and the EYFS. The practitioners' interactions will be analysed with the SSTEW (Shared Sustained, Emotional, and Well-being scale). By the end of the project, we will produce a training booklet supported by video clips and, most importantly, hope to see a sustained impact on practitioners' confidence in facilitating language and thinking and improvement in children's use of language for thinking and engagement with stories. There are also plans to integrate these resources into all early years of training courses at the university.

NEARLY CAUGHT.

Chapter 2 – Philosophical Babies

Babies are born as natural philosophers. All they have is 'why?'. They have spent nine months with dulled and filtered lights and noises. The loudest noise they have heard is the constant, predictable beat of their mum's heart and *swoosh, swoosh* of her bloodstream. After birth, this lasts for mere seconds. Then suddenly, without warning, they are thrust into the world; the noisy, bright, chaotic world full of sights, sounds, and assaults to the senses. (LISTEN/LOOK) They have no preconceptions, no opinions, no language.

Babies instantly begin to soak in the world. It starts with the essential pieces of knowledge – that hurts, that feels nice, that is interesting. The longer they are in the world, the more they soak in and digest. Soon they learn who their special people are (GROUP), what to do when they are hungry, that their voice makes a sound, and that sound makes people react (TEST/VARY). Before you know it, the gurgles, coos, and social smiles come, and Hey Presto! You have a mini human ready to learn about the world. They are even already starting to demonstrate the Thinking Moves all on their own, as you can see when I reference them throughout this chapter. As they watch their parent unbutton their top or mix up some formula, they already know what this means; food. Already they are using the Thinking Move **AHEAD**. Sure you won't get a Socrates-worthy enquiry out of them. More likely to get a bit of milky vomit and a loose nappy. You do, however, have a tiny sponge which is ready to learn. It is a perfect time to start building a mini-Plato.

You fuel their curiosities every day by introducing new experiences, new tastes, textures, smells, and sounds. You build their vestibular and proprioceptive awareness as you hug them tight, wrap them up, bounce them on your knee and carry them around. You develop their language as you speak and sing to them. You build their sense of the imaginary as you use silly voices. You show them that their vocalisations have a purpose and effect as you respond to their cries or copy their sounds (RESPOND/CONNECT). This is the time when tiny humans learn that their voice has power. It is the time where they first begin to make personal and social connections. They start to learn the certainties of the world; hunger, temperature, light, noise, voices (GROUP); but they do not yet have any preconceived notions or ideas about the world. They are an open book waiting for us to write in. It is at this point that we can make the active decision to feed their fire of inquisitiveness with everything we can offer them. To begin their philosophical journey, we can make sure that they spend time looking at faces – ours or other people's. We mirror their facial expressions (CONNECT). We pull happy faces, sad faces, angry faces (DIVIDE).

We explore different sights, sounds, and textures (TEST). We introduce different tastes when they are ready for food (VARY)– perhaps opting for baby-led weaning where an awful lot of problem-solving goes into your baby figuring out how to get that food to their mouth (TEST/USE/VARY). Through all of this, we talk, throwing every word we know at them (EXPLAIN). We don't dumb down what we say in the hope it will be more readily understood. We use all of our words because if a child does not hear them, they will not learn them.

If a six-month-old baby does not understand "happy girl" anyway, then what harm will it be to say instead "You are such a happy girl. You are smiling, so I know you are happy"? The same message (HEADLINE) with the same keywords (KEYWORD) emphasised (and repeated). Now with thirteen other words used and a linking explanation – *you are happy, and I know that because you are smiling* (INFER/JUSTIFY). Let's give our babies those new words when we can. Not all the time, of course. As parents or practitioners, we don't have time (in our boring adult world) to be keeping up that level of pre-meditated talk all the time. After all, there are dishes to be done and assessments to be highlighted, but we can do it more.

During their first three years, a child's brain triples in weight and establishes about 1,000 trillion nerve connections, and this starts from this very moment they are born. Here are some ways that we are already making our babies into philosophers. As I said, you are already doing it; you just need to reframe your thinking a little bit to realise HOW you are doing it.

Philosophical Skill – Curiosity

The parietal lobe in the babies' brains makes them primed to begin to learn about the sensory aspects of their world (LISTEN/LOOK). You help babies develop their sense of curiosity in everything you introduce them to, and there is no better place to start than with their basic physical senses. Work on their physical senses with messy play, hand painting, feeling different textures, baby massage, and tasting new foods once they have started weaning (TEST/VARY). Baby's occipital lobe controls visual awareness – what a baby sees and begins to recognise. As babies are naturally short-sighted when they are born, keep this in mind. When you talk to baby, be near to their face. When you show them new things, hold them close.

By six months baby will have much better eyesight, much more control of their eyes and head, and have much more awareness of 'things' as they have catalogued six months' worth of knowledge of the world and visual recognition in their minds. Continue to show them new sights, patterns, and bold colours (GROUP/VARY). Introduce sensory curiosities such as glitter jars, lava lamps, and in sensory rooms (ZOOM). Ignite the curiosity of their temporal lobe by introducing new smells, sounds, and tastes all the time (VARY). You already have a curious little philosopher who is ready to explore the world.

Philosophical Skill – Language

To support your baby's language development all you need to do is communicate with them; talk, sing songs, tell stories and use the tone of your voice to convey emotion and different character voices (PICTURE). Point things out and name them all the time (KEYWORD). You should choose when it is appropriate to use one or two words to teach a basic concept ("Look. Cat!") (HEADLINE) and when you can introduce more language and complex sentences. Seize opportunities to feed the baby's ears with the music of new vocabulary ("Look – the cat is jumping onto the wall. Wow! Good jump cat!") (HEADLINE/EXPLAIN). You don't have to work your way up from the basics to the complex over a long period of time.– you are, instead, creating a rich tapestry of language where you weave both simple and complex sentences into your daily life.

Philosophical Skill – Listening

Hearing is a passive skill (for those of us lucky enough not to be hearing impaired) which baby has been already using for many months before they are even born. Listening effectively is an active skill, and it is one we can teach from a young age. Sing songs and hold the baby so that they are watching your mouth move as well as listening to your voice (LISTEN/LOOK). Vary your voice – loud/quiet, deep/high, etc. (VARY). Play music – folk music, rock music, classical music, rap music, music from around the world (DIVIDE). If you are bilingual or multilingual use all of your languages with the baby. Get your baby attuned to every sound, tone, and syllable the world has to offer.

Philosophical Skill – Social Awareness and Higher-Level Thinking

Between the ages of six-twelve months, the development of the frontal lobe really begins to progress, meaning that baby is starting to create their own understanding and explorations of language, problem-solving and social awareness (EXPLAIN/FORMULATE). In addition, the cerebellum, as well as helping baby to navigate their balance and movements, opens up the world of higher-level thinking.

Social awareness and higher-level thinking are things which babies will become more skilled in as they get older; however, it all starts now. Help the baby to understand emotion by showing them different faces and emotions and naming them (CONNECT/DIVIDE/KEYWORD). Model the faces yourself, show them photographs and pictures, name their feelings when they are experiencing them (LISTEN/LOOK/INFER/EXEMPLIFY).

Help baby to understand social interaction by seeing you talk to and interact with the people around you – children and adults. Have a conversation with your baby by using intensive interaction. If your baby coos, copy the coo. If the baby makes any noise, copy it right back. Teach your baby the unspoken rules of interaction – if you make a noise, I will make one back (QUESTION/RESPOND). We are interacting and having a conversation – your words and sounds have power, and I want to be a part of your world and invite you to be a part of mine (CONNECT).

So did I teach you anything you don't already know? Did I tell you to do anything you aren't already doing as a parent or Early Years practitioner? I thought not.

That is the beauty of a philosophical, and Thinking Moves, approach to pedagogy. For the most part, you are already doing it and have been for some time. You just need to reframe your thinking a bit, that is all. The benefit of it is that, for the first time, you can see and appreciate that all of the things you are doing naturally are so important and are helping to create metacognative skills. As all parents and practitioners know, we are never 'just playing'; we are building brains. What you do every day is powerful and makes a real significant impact, and hopefully, this book will show you that.

As you read on, you will see that some of the Thinking Moves you already do. That is how intuitive and natural they are. Some of the moves will take more thought and are not accessible to babies, however, this should not stop you from practising the skill as they are useful to help us, adults, to form a metacognition framework for the way we communicate with babies as their little brains and understanding of the world grows.

Chapter 3 - Thinking Moves With Babies

A -AHEAD

Thinking ahead is a skill that is in most children from a young age, even if only thinking ahead or being able to anticipate by a few seconds. If you watch a young baby who is about to have a bottle, their mouth will open before the bottle reaches its mouth. Baby is showing that they can anticipate what is going to happen and looking a second into the future. Although babies are not born with these skills, it is something that develops quite early and is a natural skill to help build within your regular daily routine. Talk about what you are going to do today as you greet them in the morning. As you dress the child or change their nappy tell them what you will be doing next in the process. Talk about set times of the day as they approach. In a nursery setting, this may be things like nursery rhyme time and home time. At home, it would be your plans for the day. The Thinking Move of **AHEAD** really is as intuitive and straightforward as it sounds.

B – BACK

The ability to think back is often more natural than that of thinking ahead, making it a great move to do with babies. It is talking about something which has already happened, reminding the baby of it, and talking it through to help make sense of it. Throughout the day you can talk about what has just occurred "Oh! The ball rolled away", "Someone rang the doorbell". When they do something, repeat it back to them, "You smiled" "You laughed".

In such early life, the time difference between an event and referencing the event might only be a few seconds, making this move a very close relative of **LISTEN/LOOK**. To begin to build the skill up further, you can talk about things that happened a little bit further in the past. If you are in a nursery or a childminder, make it a habit to talk about what you did that day as you wait for home time.

C – CONNECT

The skill of **CONNECT** is based on looking for similarities. This is a skill that is inherently a part of early childhood as children learn to label and categorise items (making this move a natural prerequisite for (GROUP). You can support this skill by looking at things that are the same (connected in some way) and verbally labelling them. For example, have a collection of red things and play with them together, repeating the word 'red'.

GROUP things by type and relation to show **CONNECT** in the broader sense, e.g. cats. Look at pictures of cats and ideas associated with cats (bowls, balls of string, cat eyes, drawings of cats, photos of cats). You can use this approach to make themed baskets (cats, babies, seaside, teddy bears, silver kitchen utensils, etc.).

CONNECT is also a lovely skill for instilling those views of the world that I talked about in the introduction; learning what connects all humans rather than what divides them. A great resource to use is a baby photo book. You can buy these picture books or make your own from photos from magazines or the internet. By having children of all races, differently-abled children and children who are not signified as being, male or female by their clothing, you can focus instead on pointing out things about each baby to show how we are all connected. "That baby is laughing. You laugh when I tickle you" "Look, that baby is playing with bricks like yours" and so on.

You can also show them their voice has power by playing games in which you respond to their voice, for example by holding a toy in front of them and whenever baby makes a noise you wobble or shake the toy. This starts to teach them the cause and effect of using their voice. Create social connections by copying the vocalisations the baby makes to teach them that you are connected in the same world, and your interactions connect you as people. For young babies and older children with additional needs and communication barriers, this is closely similar to an Intensive Interaction approach (https://www.intensiveinteraction.org/).

D – DIVIDE

It is a natural progression to go from **CONNECT** to **DIVIDE**. **DIVIDE** could be said to be **CONNECT'S** contrary sibling, and it is difficult to do one without the other. After all, how can a baby begin to understand what 'soft' is if they do not know 'hard' to compare it to? **DIVIDE** can often be more accessible at this age than **CONNECT,** and there are many things you can do. Look at different things such as the same toy in different colours (simple toys like building blocks are a good start) or different animal toys and label them "this is a dog", "this is a cow". Babies do not need more than two items. Pace yourself.

Look at opposites in all parts of the day. Lift baby high in the air and say "up" then down low and say "down". You can also do this with song, e.g. The Grand Old Duke of York. As you wipe baby's face with a wet cloth or wet wipe, say "wet" then as you dry them say "dry". Explore this through washing and drying the baby's hand or, as they get older, engaging in sensory play with wet and dry items. Much like with Connect, you could make Divide exploration baskets; rough/smooth, black/white, big/small, etc.).

E – EXPLAIN

Though this is a natural move when children get older (and start to answer back), it is one that we often forget to do with young babies. It's a skill that is easy but one that we need to remind ourselves to do until it becomes a habit actively. Throughout the day, talk about what you are doing or what the baby is doing. Use the Hanen Programme® *Learning Language and Loving It™* (www.hanen.org/Home.aspx) approach by explaining things and saying what baby would say if they could, e.g. "Oh! You are crying because you are hungry" "You are giggling because that tickled". Explain what you are doing too; "I am tidying up the toys now" "I am putting my coat on." As baby approaches age one, look out for more regular 'explaining' from your baby as they start to point to things that they want.

F – FORMULATE

To support this move, provide baby with toys they can try to formulate their plans to get to or reach for e.g. Toys dangling above their baby bouncer or toys just out of their reach at tummy time. When just about to feed them hover that bottle or spoon for a couple of extra seconds so that baby can formulate how to get the food. Will they reach for it? Will they cry or look pointedly at you? As baby starts to sit up, provide toys that have a problem-solving element. Sit or lie with them on the floor and let them lead the way as they experiment with trial and error until they figure the toy out.

G – GROUP

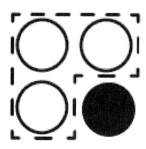

Grouping is a great way to begin to understand the world and how things can relate to each other.

You can group items with baby by types such as soft toys and hard toys, big things, and small things. Talk about each group as you do it. Remember that you only need two or three things in each group for such a young child.

You can also talk to baby as you sort washing, go shopping, or tidy up as you group things by type. Grouping is something which will become more comfortable and more varied as your baby reaches the toddler years.

H – HEADLINE

Talk about what you have done in short sentences such as "We have made milk to drink" or "We are getting in the car to go to the shop". Give headlines about what you see "It is raining today" or hear "The dog is saying woof".

I – INFER

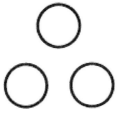

Talk about what has happened and what that means, e.g. "Oh! The doorbell rang. Someone must be at the door", "You smiled, you must be happy". A slightly different but similar skill will be anticipating. You can sing anticipation songs that end in a drop or tickle such as Round and Round the Garden or games like Peekaboo so that baby can start to anticipate and infer from your pauses that you are about to do something.

J – JUSTIFY

When you talk to baby justify why you are doing things, e.g. "I am putting your socks on to keep your feet warm" or "The cat is meowing because she needs some food". Justify things you can't do too "I can't get you out of the car seat because we are driving" "You can't have that because it is dangerous".

K – KEYWORD

Label things as you look at them. Use as few words as possible to make it clear that you are naming things and not using any of the other skills. You can do this for objects (for example saying "tree" every time you pass a tree), a single object (showing baby the same ball over and over while saying "ball"), people (looking through a photo album and naming a few people), actions ("clap clap" as you clap hands) or emotions (smile and say "happy"). When having a cuddle, you can also do this with flashcards or picture books.

L – LISTEN/LOOK

Looking and listening are things which baby does more of every day as their physical abilities and curiosity grow. You can explore different musical instruments. Listening walks are also a lovely part of a daily routine. As you walk with the pram stop to listen whenever you hear an unusual noise. Play with voice sounds. Sing songs. Point to pictures in books. Play with sensory lighting and objects that spin. Get baby used to you saying the words "Look!" and Listen!" then pointing out something of interest. Listening walks can be done outdoors or indoors.

M – MAINTAIN

Teach baby the word "yes" and say it as you play games, e.g., "Is this your tummy? Yes! Is this your nose? Yes", nodding your head as you say yes.

N – NEGATE

Teach baby the word "no" by playing hide and seek with a favourite toy under a blanket. Say, "Is teddy in my hand? No. Is teddy up my top? No. Is teddy on my head? No. Where is teddy? Here he is!" as you finally lift the blanket. As baby gets older and more adventurous (and cheeky), say no and shake your head whenever you need to. Encourage older babies to begin to copy you and nod or shake their head and learn to say yes (**MAINTAIN**) and no (**NEGATE**) themselves.

O – ORDER

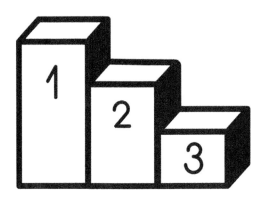

Babies will not have this thinking skill or get it for a long time, but that doesn't mean you can't introduce it in play as a way to teach new vocabulary. Start small now to make this a habit by the time baby turns into an older toddler.

You can use ordinal language as you do everyday things to introduce the concept of things having an order. "First we will take your nappy off, next/secondly we will wipe your bottom, then/thirdly we will put some cream on, finally/last of all we will put your new nappy on."

Do it in even simpler forms throughout the day. "First, we will put you in your pram; then we will go on a walk."

You could also do this in a more specific activity, for example, ordering three teddy bears as you say their sizes "Small, big, bigger."

P – PICTURE

We are now with another Thinking Move that will not be developmentally possible for a baby; however, this doesn't stop you from practising the move yourself and using it as a way to structure your chat.

At this early stage, you could combine this with AHEAD or BACK to talk about things that are not happening in the present.

You could also use it to give context to vocabulary, e.g., "that is a cat. Cats can be brown or black, orange or white. Cats can climb trees," and so on.

You are also laying the groundwork for this skill every time you talk about someone who isn't in the room, and every time you sing a nursery rhyme or read a story. This is an essential step in teaching babies about the world around them, both that they can see and that they can't.

Q – QUESTION and R – RESPOND

When was the last time a three-month-old baby asked you a question? Not recently, right? But when was the last time you asked a baby a question or heard someone else doing it?

We use questions (and RESPOND) all the time with babies. Every day we say the things that they cannot say themselves. We QUESTION, "Are you hungry?" "All better now?" "What's wrong baby?" even though we know the baby can't answer.

We also RESPOND to their actions, vocalisations, and expressions. Babies soon learn to respond to us, too, as they become more focused on our voices and faces and start to react to or mirror our expressions and noises.

So to help you become an expert in these two Thinking Moves, all I need to say is... keep on doing what you are doing. You are already an expert.

S – SIZE

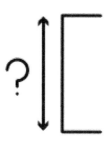

Back into a more easily done Thinking Move now. This move is one which we do with babies instinctively all the time.

From pointing things out, "Look at that big tree," to little games such as stretching the baby's arms up and saying "so big!" If you don't already do it (I am sure you do), then add the language of size into your everyday chat and show baby things that are big and small.

This is an excellent time to add in some weights and measures too, such as talking about full and empty (bottles, spoons, etc.) or heavy and light ("You are getting bigger. You are getting so heavy!"). You can also introduce the language of time such as "We will have a cuddle for a minute".

T – TEST and U – USE

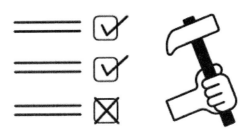

Back in the realm of more stretching moves, these become easier when baby gets older, but, as you have now discovered, it is never too early for us to help build those exciting little connections in the babies' brains. To support these Thinking Moves, use the words **TEST** and **USE** explicitly when you do things. "Let's test the bottle to see if your milk is too warm. I will use the back of my hand to test it." "I will test the bathwater to see if it is just right. I will use my elbow" "Let's test your new socks. We will try them on to see if they fit." **(USE)** You will see babies test things out and use what they learn in everyday life too. Just watch any baby who is learning to roll over, crawl, or walk, and you will see the ultimate analytical scientist.

V – VARY

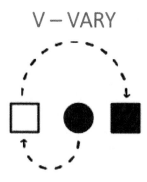

Once babies can sit upright (either in a bouncer/ high chair or independently), **VARY** becomes a smooth Thinking Move to explore through play. You could build towers of blocks, and when they fall down, say, "oh no! It fell down because... Let's vary how we do it." Or play a peekaboo game with toys by putting three toys on the highchair tray and taking a different toy away each time and talking about it. "A ball, a cup, and a teddy. Where has the teddy gone? Here he is – peekaboo!" You can also do this during everyday life once the baby starts weaning as you vary the different textures and flavours of food. By introducing new textures, you are helping the baby's brain get used to variations in taste and texture. By changing the thing you wipe baby with in the bath (flannels, sort cotton, baby wipes, sponges), you are introducing varying textures on baby's skin.

W – WEIGH UP

In Early Years terms, weighing up simply means to choose. Choosing may be more of a toddler skill than a baby one, but it is never too young to give a choice. When a baby is very small, it will be a case of holding two things up and verbally choosing between them yourself, "Should I put you in the blue vest or the orange one? I think we will choose the orange one", but as the baby gets slightly older, they can begin to choose on their own.

Try holding up two toys and asking, "Which one do you want?" At a first level, you will see the baby's eyes and attention focus on one item in particular, but as they get older, they will begin to reach for the toy they want and even vocalise actively.

As an extension, once they start shuffling then crawling, you will regularly begin to see baby weigh up their options, then set their sights on the object (or person) they want and go for it!

X – eXEMPLIFY

A bit of a tricky one here, but it is possible to see how babies can do this as they get a bit older. One example would be baby looking at pictures of animals and making animal noises as their adult points to them, therefore giving their example of what they think each animal is.

Sticking with the picture book theme, invest in books that have examples of one specific thing on each page. There are so many of these to choose from, and you probably already own some. Common examples are rainbow books that have lots of items of just one colour on each page or books with a page dedicated to vehicles. "These are types of vehicles. Those vehicles are cars, and those vehicles are boats, etc.". You could also team this with **GROUP** as you sort toys into types.

Y – YIELD

Admittedly yielding is not a skill that babies and toddlers are known for. Three to five-year-olds are more able to do this with support. For babies, it will be more of a case of learning turn-taking. Yielding to someone else's turn to speak as they learn the rules of conversation would be an example, so when the baby is burbling and vocalising, interrupt them to copy their sounds, make a new one, or say words. Then you yield and wait for them to make more sounds. Carry this on as you have a conversation with them. You will also see yielding once babies start weaning onto solid foods. If the baby doesn't like a taste or texture the first time they try a new type of food, then don't give up on it immediately. Instead, offer this new food several more times in the future to see if they yield and start to like it.

Not liking broccoli

Z – ZOOM

Babies have much less developed eyesight than older children, so zooming out may not be possible. Likewise, they do not have the same capacity to focus on small details. The best approach for supporting this Thinking Move for young babies is to have lots of face to face time so that baby can focus on your face. As they get older, introduce toys and pictures with bright or bold prints (particularly high contrast colours like black and white) and toys that move, such as mobiles and spinning toys.

So there you go! I bet you never believed that all 26 Thinking Moves would be relevant to a baby who can't even talk yet, did you? It is at this point that I want to give you a huge reminder and reassurance. Do not worry too much about the Thinking Moves words. If you aren't using them with babies and toddlers, then do not worry. If your three to five-year-olds don't use or know how to use the words, then do not worry.

Thinking Moves for older children can be more explicit and prescriptive, but for children under five, it is not a tick list of things that every child needs to memorise. Think of it more as a way of thinking for you to make sure you are helping children to develop every part of their magnificent little brains at the point in their lives where the most neural connections are forming. You may not see the impact of what you are doing, but you can bet it is happening.

Chapter 4 – Philosophical Toddlers

Ah, toddlers. Tiny little dictators with great big emotions. At the time of writing this, I have three children, all boys, and all philosophers in their way. However, I currently wish that I hadn't taught the teenagers how to think creatively and critically as they now use it against me whenever something is up for debate (or not!). Their youngest brother is currently four years old and so, along with the three and four-year-olds that I teach, the toddler years are something still vividly in my memory. It is now, with these two different age groups, that I have begun to see why my mother's greatest curse to me when I was growing up was *"I hope that one day you have a child who is JUST like you!"*.

If you are reading this book, then I am assuming that you too are proactively bringing up your own child or teaching a class of children to be "just like you" also.

It is the toddler years where you first get a glimpse of a child's real personality. They have done their learning about how to be alive and survive. They have learnt so much over the first two years of their life and now (oh no!) they have learnt that they are a master of their own fate. DON'T BE SCARED! You are bigger than them. You know more. You have got this, ok? But all of these frustrating things that our toddlers do are evidence of their metacognitive brains at work.

They want to climb the bookcase? They are just curious about what is at the top (SIZE). They want to throw their food across the floor then look at you in defiance? They are just cataloguing your reaction (GROUP/ORDER). They throw a toy at your head? They are exploring boundaries (WEIGH UP). They have a 10-minute meltdown in the alcohol aisle of Tesco because you won't let them carry a bottle of gin they have just pulled off the shelf? They are exploring emotions and how long they can say 'no' before they have to give in (MAINTAIN/NEGATE/YIELD). They show absolutely no remorse at smearing your brand new, expensive concealer on a table because they were experimenting with painting (yes, that was my middle child) (MAINTAIN/USE/TEST). Are all of these things acceptable? Of course not. Should you allow them in the name of philosophy? Nope. These are just examples to show you that children are already full of the curiosity and skills of philosophy from an early age.

Toddlers are entering such a fantastic phase of childhood. They go from being little sponges who pleasantly take in the world around them to independent, stubborn, willful, excitable souls. They have extremes of emotion. They are so delighted that their knees go wobbly from laughter. They are so excited that they squeal. They run and spin as fast as they can. They are so angry that they have to scream and kick and throw things. They are so devastated that they sob their heart out with big fat tears rolling down their cheeks and a "why, why, why?" look on their little face. They are so in love that they cannot bear to not be in physical contact with you or a beloved toy. They are so filled with hate that if the cat comes any closer, they will pull its tail and shout "NO CAT" at it (NEGATE/MAINTAIN). Toddlers are discovering all of the emotions that the world has to offer. All those emotions you have spent the last two years teaching them about are now being experienced, and they understand the words you use to describe them but cannot yet manage them (KEYWORD/HEADLINE).

It is around this age that toddlers get a hold of imaginary play too (PICTURE). They have little adventures with figures or cars, and they make you pretend cups of tea or use boxes as boats. They take all of the things they have seen on television or heard in stories and build the storylines, narratives, characters, and situations into their play (USE). They are beginning to learn about what is real but also have the ability to imagine other 'realities' and put themselves into different character roles as they start to learn and practice empathy. A lot of their role play is based on things they have seen or experienced themselves, and this is a philosophical skill too – to build up opinions and a bank of knowledge based on your own experiences (AHEAD/BACK/FORMULATE).

Toddlers are problem solvers too. They get a car stuck in a play garage and will try different ways to get it out (TEST/VARY). They want a biscuit from a shelf in the cupboard so will drag something over to climb up and get it. They begin to try to dress and undress with just a bit of help. They figure out emotional problem solving as they manipulate adults into behaving the way they want them to. They can look at a toy that they want at the bottom of their toy box and can anticipate different possible approaches, scenarios, and outcomes, on a basic level, as they figure out how to get to the said toy (ZOOM/FORMULATE/VARY).

As before a lot of what you already do as a practitioner or parent will be forming your child into a philosopher, but here are a few hints and tips.

Philosophical Skill – Language Development

Again this is a time not to dumb down the language you use. Of course, there will be times where you need to make your use of language short and efficient to get a specific result (HEADLINE) but more often than not you will be able to use the full extent of language that you would naturally use with an older child to explain things (EXPLAIN) and also expand on the why of things (JUSTIFY). Remember that this is the time when children are rapidly learning new words and phrases, more so than at any other time in their life, so bless them with every word in your mental closet and build great little communicators. Keep on telling those stories and singing those songs.

Children of this age have a deeper understanding of language than we often give them credit for. A child might have just a few phrases, but that does not mean that they have only a few meanings. For example, as a toddler, my youngest went through a phase of saying "oh dear", but to him, this meant a world of things. He used it when he fell, or something terrible happened to mean 'I'm sad'. He used it when he did something wrong on purpose, like throwing a toy in anger (sarcastic child!). He used it when he dropped something. He used it as an accusation and accompanied by a glare when someone did something he didn't like. It was one phrase made up of just two words, but to him, it could mean many different things (GROUP/CONNECT/DIVIDE/EXPLAIN).

Philosophical Skill – Problem Solving and Making Choices

Toddlers are very good at making choices (WEIGH UP). This toy or that, this snack or that. The decision is usually made so quickly that it is evident that they are going with their gut feeling or for their favourite with only a bit of thought, but even then, they are learning. They are actively looking at two options, very quickly weighing them up and making a choice (LISTEN/LOOK/WEIGH UP/MAINTAIN). Once they are good at this extend choices to three items – which pair of shoes, which biscuit, etc. In doing this, you are giving them the philosophical skill of considering three different options, weighing up the pros and cons, and making a choice, even if only on a fundamental level.

Philosophical Skill – Question Words

Question words are one of the essential tools for a facilitator when introducing and supporting a philosophical enquiry. Question words are not always easily understood by toddlers and do sit more comfortably in the realm of pre-schoolers; however, it is never too early to begin to model these skills (QUESTION).

Introduce the words 'why/because'. These are difficult for even three-year-olds to understand, so get started now. You will have to model it a lot for it to be understood so make this a long term project. "Why did you choose that biscuit? Oh, I know. It is because it has chocolate on it." **(EXPLAIN/JUSTIFY)** "Why did you choose the welly boots? Is it because you want to jump in puddles?" **(INFER/QUESTION)**

I have found that for the age group we work with, the two words with the most useful power in philosophy are 'why' and 'because' and they are relatively easy to teach when a child reaches three and four. Getting started now gives all of that underlying modelling before you expect the children to start using the words themselves.

Philosophical Skill – Imagination and Awareness

Toddlers who are developing at a typical rate will now have object permanence. They will realise that things exist even if they cannot see them **(PICTURE/AHEAD/BACK)**. They know that mummy or daddy are not there but that they still exist somewhere – they are off shopping or at work, they are in the kitchen or the other room. It is now that you can nurture this awareness of counter realities and so build a child who can philosophise.

When someone is not there, talk about them **(EXPLAIN/eXEMPIFY/PICTURE)**. Tell the children what they are doing and where. Build this invisible world outside of what the child can see there and then. This doesn't have to be about people the child knows. It could be about occupations. "Right now a doctor is helping a little boy", "The postman is probably dropping letters off at all of the houses in your street right now", and so on **(PICTURE/HEADLINE)**.

Philosophical Skill – Counter Realities

Toddlers acquire a new skill that they did not have as babies; imagination. They have learnt enough about the real world, from the things they have seen and experienced, and the imaginary world, from books and cartoons, to begin to reenact and create their own scenarios **(AHEAD/BACK/PICTURE)**. Many toddlers cannot yet hold conversations, but they can act out whole adventures with tiny toys, complete with bursts of phrases like "Ahoy shipmate!" and "I go in the deep dark wood" (FORMULATE/USE). They already have rich imaginations and, with it, the ability to imagine different possible realities, outcomes, and situations (PICTURE/VARY). They are philosophising 'what ifs' all the time to come up with tiny adventures. When toddlers become stubborn and start to test the boundaries (MAINTAIN/NEGATE), they are also exploring counter realities. What will happen if...? (TEST) They are developing a beginner's knowledge of cause and effect that extends past that of 'if I drop this ball what will happen?' and into the realm of human scenarios.

As toddlers are still very egocentric, these scenarios will be based more on 'what can I get away with?' than 'how will this make someone feel' but they are making their first steps towards moral philosophy for sure. To help them with this development, join in their play (eXEPLIFY). Let them control the imaginary worlds as they explore their understanding, for example, as they serve you your imaginary fourth cup of tea of the day, change the game (VARY). Look in the cup and say 'Yuk! Worms! I don't want worms!'. See how they react when the outcome is not what they anticipated (YIELD). After ten minutes of playing with Peppa Pig toys, probably reenacting a scene from a favourite episode over and over again, introduce the Big Bad Wolf to the game and see what happens (VARY). Can they use what they know about the Big Bad Wolf to create a new storyline? (BACK/FORMULATE)

Now I will ask you the question again. Was any of this new to you? Were any of these things which were so alien that you never even considered doing them? I am betting not. As you will be beginning to realise, doing a focused Philosophy for Children session takes planning and practice, but having a philosophical ethos and approach to teaching is probably something you are already doing. You just never knew it.

Chapter 5 – Thinking Moves With Toddlers

Now that you are familiar with how Thinking Moves worked with babies, the progression to using this philosophical thinking approach with toddlers should be smooth. The most significant change will be when children enter the age of three to five years old. For now, there is just a small graduation in skills and ability from the baby years. You will find that the main change is that children become more able to join in and interact with activities and discussion, in their own little toddler ways.

A -AHEAD

Similar to with babies, the easiest way to practice thinking **AHEAD** is to talk about what you will be doing later in the day. As toddlers are now old hands at peekaboo style games, they have built up the skill of anticipating. This means that games such as blowing balloons and popping bubbles, as well as songs such as Round and Round the Garden and This Little Piggy. You could also play games where you swoop your child into the air or drop them down a little bit as part of a rhyme which will foster their love of looking just a tiny bit into the future to anticipate a fun sensory input. Talking about daily events will help too as you ask questions about what your toddler would like for a snack or meal later and where you should go on your afternoon trip out. It is a great time to introduce future tense words, such as 'next', 'later', 'soon', 'tonight', and 'tomorrow'.

B – BACK

An excellent way of thinking **BACK** is to have conversations about what happened earlier in the day or the day before. Introduce past tense words such as, 'before', 'this morning', and 'yesterday'.

Each afternoon or evening, talk about everything that happened that day.

 You can also use this as a teaching moment for safety or behaviour, for example, 'Do you remember last time you pulled the cat's tail? She tried to scratch you' or 'Remember that last time you threw your food on the floor it had to go in the bin'.

C – CONNECT and D-DIVIDE

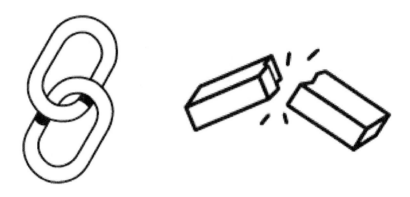

These skills are very hard to separate when working with such young children, so they are often best together.

To build these skills, you can carry on with the tasks done with babies but expect the child to interact more. Sorting toys is a great way to do this as you tidy into different baskets. As you sort, give your toddler more of a free rein to do the sorting themselves. Demonstrate for the first few items then let your toddler try, supporting them when they sort incorrectly.

You can start to use the Thinking Moves words at this point. For example "We are going to sort our things out. We will divide them into books in this basket and toys in that basket" once finished "Hurray! All of the things in that basket are connected because they are toys. All of the things in that basket are connected because they are books".

Your toddler now has a better grasp of language and is starting to pay attention to other children. It is a good time to revisit the activity we did with the babies and look at photo books of babies and children to talk about the things that connect us all as humans.

Don't worry if you feel silly saying the Thinking Moves words to your toddler. If you feel too foolish then just don't say them. The main point at this stage is to learn the skill, not the word. The word can come later.

E – EXPLAIN

Now that your toddler has begun to say some words (and as they get closer to three years, some short sentences) it is time for this Thinking Move to really come into its own. As you continue to explain things to your toddler throughout the day, you can now expect that they will also begin to explain things to you. From which toy or comfort item they want to how they hurt their finger, the explanations will come thick and fast from your toddler. You can encourage this further by sometimes playing ignorant. For example, you may know perfectly well that what they are reaching for is their favourite blankie but encourage them to use their words, and the power of their words, by saying "What do you want? Explain to me, and I will get it for you".

As you will see in this example, I used the Thinking Move word EXPLAIN, and it seemed quite natural in the sentence. As this is a word we regularly use every day, it is one which you will be able to use yourself confidently to support this thinking skill.

F – FORMULATE

If you think about an average day in the life of a toddler, you will realise that they spend a lot of their time formulating. They routinely try to figure out how to get into or out of places they shouldn't be in or how to get things that are too high for them. They work out how to get your attention or get their own way. Although they do it in a very egocentric way, our little manipulators are already experts at this Thinking Move. It is time for us to step in and teach them how to use this power for good.

For activities that fit well into developing this Thinking Move, think about puzzle-solving games. Shape sorting games and jigsaw puzzles are a good start. Verbally ask your toddler for their ideas and opinions as you ask "What should we do today?" or "How can we get teddy down from the shelf?"

G – GROUP

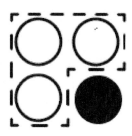

Grouping is a skill that most toddlers won't have yet but is one that they are now developmentally ready to begin to learn.

Grouping is such an easy activity to be done and can be done with anything at any time; food on a plate, packets, and tins, cats and dogs, red and blue. From a safety point of view, it can also mean things you can do and things you can't or items you are allowed to touch and things you shouldn't touch. As you are now becoming experts, you will have spotted the natural links with **CONNECT** and **DIVIDE** here too.

Grouping is a natural activity to do, is easy to learn and, once learnt, opens the door to so many other skills.

H – HEADLINE

The key to headlining is to be able to distil complex information or a large amount of data into a very brief overview. We do this all the time with toddlers due to their level of development and understanding. While we might say to an older child "Don't play there. There is a hot coffee on the table, and it might get knocked over and burn you", to a toddler we might say "No! Hot! Ouch!" as we point to the cup and act out getting burnt. To get a message across we have simplified it into a headline.

I did say, earlier in this book, that when the opportunity presents itself, we should throw as many words as we can at children to support them, gaining an understanding of a broad vocabulary. There is a time to do that, but there are also many times where a headline is more impactful and useful.

To create specific opportunities to headline, you could look at picture books. Instead of reading the words, try to reduce the content of the page into a headline. So instead of "Once upon a time there were three little pigs who lived in a lovely house with their mother", headline it as "Three pigs lived with their mummy".

I – INFER

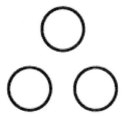

As children move from being babies to toddlers, they begin to learn how to infer things. It will not be unusual to see a child doing this naturally and without support. It is a testament to your incredible skills as a practitioner or parent that they have built up so much experience from your interactions with them.

We have talked already about a hot cup of coffee. This headlining will follow through to an ability to infer. For example, a cautious toddler may have no qualms about trying to pick up a full glass of water or juice; however, they may altogether avoid picking up a cup because past experience has taught them to infer that the contents will be hot. They may see you pull your bottom lip out or turn the corners of your mouth down and will try to cuddle you or stroke your face as they infer that this means you are sad. Your toddler may see you getting cutlery out of a drawer and then respond in a way that makes it clear to you that they have inferred that it is lunchtime.

To help to build the skill of inference, you could try several activities with your child. Put two plastic cups (different colours) upside down. Show your child as you place a toy under one cup then move them around and lift the cup as you say "it was under the blue cup". Repeat several times with the toy under the same cup and after a few times give your child the chance to tell you which cup it is under.

Once your toddler gets good at this inferring, you could move onto the Thinking Move **VARY** and change which cup the toy is under to make it into a guessing game.

INFER also works well with **CONNECT,** and you could play games where you look at different habitats and match up who lives where. For example pictures of different houses with clues about their inhabitants. Which animal lives in the house with a bone on the door? Which one lives in the house with a fish tank in the window? Your toddler will not have the skills to do this independently yet, but as you talk through each picture and who lives there (and how you know) they will begin to see and get used to how to **INFER.**

J – JUSTIFY

Toddlers are the absolute masters and mistresses of this skill. From the minute they learn to argue back, they are justifying. It might not always be adult logic but, from their point of view, the justifications make sense. Our job is to teach them how to make their reasons more logical. You can begin to model this skill when your older toddler asks "why?" Even though you will hear that word far too many times, it provides a perfect excuse to justify.

It is a great time to also introduce the word 'because' as an indicator that you are going to give a justification. Don't be afraid to ask them 'why?' too and wait for them to justify what they have done, said, or want. Try to create opportunities to justify things also. For example, if you are tidying up toys justify it, "We are tidying our toys so that they don't get lost", or "We are going to the shop because we need to buy milk".

K – KEYWORD

Toddlers are just beginning to build up their vocabulary as they enter toddlerhood. As they get closer to age three, they will start to talk in short sentences, joining two or three words together. At both of these stages, they will be using keywords to make their meaning clear. You can help to develop their use of keywords as they grow. As they turn from babies to toddlers, help them to learn the names for things. Label things as you see them in real life or pictures. As toddlers grow in understanding, link two or more keywords together. For example, go from "dog" to "big brown dog". You should also encourage your toddler to name things as you ask "what is this?"

This can be turned into a game with a lot of picture books. Give your child a keyword, and every time they see that thing, they shout the keyword out. For example model shouting "wolf" every time you see the big bad wolf in a storybook then reread the story and encourage your toddler to shout "wolf" every time they spot the wolf. The same could be done when out on a walk. Every time you spot something red, shout "red" together. This leads us nicely onto **LISTEN/LOOK.**

L – LISTEN/LOOK

You would think that listening and looking would be one of the most straightforward Thinking Moves to do with toddlers, but the tricky part is getting toddlers to look and listen to what you want them to be looking and listening to and not everything else that is going on the room. This is a Thinking Move that can easily be turned into a game though. As anyone who does Phase 1 phonics will know there are lots of listening games that can be done with children.

Going on a listening walk is always fun and an excellent opportunity to teach children about the difference between looking and listening. What can your toddler hear? A car? Well done! A red car? You can't hear red. We can hear the car, and we can see that it is red. For younger toddlers, they will not be observant or have the vocabulary enough to tell you these things but, as with everything else, you can model it. As you walk along say phrases such as "Listen, I can hear a bird, look I can see a tree" and so on. Another great Phase 1 game to play to practise looking and listening is to have two identical sets of toy instruments, such as two maracas, two bells, and two drums. Line a set up in front of you and one in front of your toddler. Encourage them to look and listen as you play one of the instruments. Can they find their instrument that looks and sounds the same?

M – MAINTAIN and N – NEGATE

Maintaining is the skill of fully committing to your own belief or view. Who better to do this than toddlers? After all, they are always right. Negating is another skill that comes naturally to toddlers as they learn to love saying "no". Often at the worst of times.

It is also a useful skill to have, though, and you can help your toddler to develop it in a more constructive way than just refusing to leave the chocolate aisle at the supermarket.

It is easiest to develop the skills of maintaining and negating when done as part of the pair. You could play a yes and no game to help your toddler begin to understand the difference between these words. Show them a picture or an item and make yes and no statements about it. For example, show your toddler a toy car and say "Do all cars have wheels? Yes. Do cars have windows? Yes. Do cars have legs? No" you could also add in less obvious statements for older toddlers such as "Are all cars red? No."

O – ORDER

Now that your baby has turned into a toddler, they are starting to get better at ordering. You may begin to see older toddlers sorting, ordering, or lining up their toys or objects. Although this will not necessarily be in an order that makes sense to an adult, you can bet that it makes logical sense to your toddler. Help them to do this in a way which is more logical by ordering things yourself and speaking as you order ("This is a small car, this is a bigger car, this is the biggest car"). Also, remember to continue with all of the ordinal languages you used with them as a baby (1st we will, then/second we will, third we will, last we will") or by standing toys in a line, one behind the other or racing toys that move (1st, second, 3rd, etc.). Lining up and building up objects is also an early skill of ordering.

P – PICTURE

When you picture things what you are doing is using the things you know plus your creativity to make an image in your head. This might be something in the past, future, something not physically present, or all manner of things from situations to feelings. Though still at a very early stage of this skill, toddlers can now begin to engage. Try talking about people who are not there. You can start with a simple question "Where is grandma?" to get your child to realise that grandma isn't there. Then move on to "What is grandma doing?" and imagine together what grandma might be doing. At this early stage 'picturing' could also be as simple as trying to get your toddler to picture anything in their mind, such as, "What do pigs look like? Are they big or small? What colour is a pig? What noise do pigs make?" as your toddler practices the skill of recalling what they know to make a picture in their mind. Picturing for toddlers and young children also includes role-play and small world play.

Q – QUESTION

By now, you will already be asking questions all the time, and sometimes getting answers. Keep on doing this and start to encourage your toddler to ask their own questions. They are most likely to do this by modelling what you say ("where's daddy?") or by asking where something is (mummy, teddy, dummy/pacifier). Though keep in mind that they will not yet be using question words, but rather saying the name of what they want ("blankie") and using facial expressions and voices to make it known what they mean. When your child does this repeat what they have said but as a question. "Where is my blankie? Here it is". Don't forget that it is never too early to model the words 'why' and 'because' as a pair during daily conversations.

For children who are almost three encourage them to take more of a lead in games where questions can be asked, for example encouraging them to say "Where are you?" When playing peekaboo or hide and seek games.

R – RESPOND

This should be a skill that your toddler has already begun to learn. You can join in with this by responding whenever your toddler speaks to you and by asking your toddler questions and leaving space for them to respond. You can also copy the noises your toddler makes or make funny or animal noises and wait for them to respond by copying you.

For older toddlers, you could sing favourite nursery rhymes but leave out the last word of another line and wait for them to say the missing word. For example, "Twinkle, twinkle, little …."

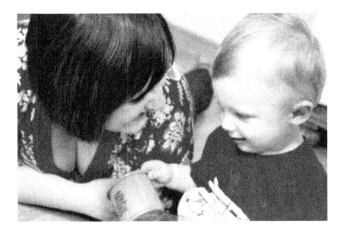

S – SIZE

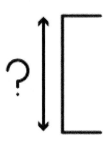

Now is a great time to begin to learn about different size words.

Your toddler will be starting to get familiar with the words "big" and "small", but now you can add in more words such as; bigger, biggest, smaller, tiny, huge, giant, miniscule. Or play with words and introduce some fun phrases like teeny weeny.

You can play with the words or attribute them to toys or the things you see.

Use the language of time too and say things like "in a minute" or "we will do this for five minutes".

T – TEST

Testing is something that you will see toddlers do all the time as they try to figure out the world. You can support this by providing lots of different open-ended problem-solving activities. Resources that would work well include; wet sand with buckets and spades, water with a variety of containers, jugs, and funnels and bottles and jars in trays of small toys which they can experiment putting in and out of the vessels. Sensory activities also work well such as; different instruments to explore, paint, sensory play such as exploring jelly, oobleck or water beads.

All of these resources can be used by toddlers to explore and verify their understanding of the world and work out how things work on their own and in relation to each other.

U – USE

Make up baskets for toddlers which are categorised by use. Examples could be different combs and brushes with a doll or soft toy with hair or fur, a toolbox with tools that would be used by a mechanic, a role play baking box. For older toddlers having open-ended loose parts to play with (cups, spoons, tubs, shells, sticks, etc.) can show you how they think as they make up different uses for them.

As young toddlers, the uses will most likely be for sensory input or to explore things such as movement, gravity, or combining. As they get older, the uses will be more likely to be as representations of real-world items and actions, for example, a tub might become a hat, and a block of plastic may become a phone.

V – VARY

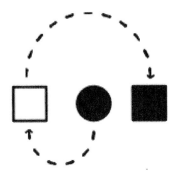

Loose parts play is also a great example of how a toddler explores 'vary'. They may pick up a stick and use it as a wand, but if you watch them for long enough, the stick will also be a fishing rod, a pole to reach something, a baby, or a walking stick. Toddlers who may not yet be able to explain the world in words will often be already learning to explain it through play.

You can also explore 'vary' through daily routines as you vary foods, different ways of presenting food, various utensils, and different trips out. When toddlers try something that just doesn't seem to be working, such as putting on their welly boots or trying to get a shape block into a shape sorter or jigsaw encourage them to persist by saying "try another way".

W – WEIGH UP

Toddlers are now old enough to make their own choices. When you are offering foods, outfits, or toys, give your toddler a choice between two options so that they can begin to build the skill of weighing up their options when making a choice. If your toddler does something wrong, then tell them that was a "bad/ wrong choice/decision" and tell them what they should have done. They may be at the age where they act impulsively, but you can still begin to teach them from this young age that they can weigh up their decisions and make a good choice. When playing with a puzzle toy or even something as simple as building a tower of bricks, give your toddler a choice of two items or approaches (one of them which is obviously wrong) so that they can begin to build up the skill of weighing things up to make a choice then see the immediate consequence/outcome.

X – eXEMPLIFY

This is a move that you will begin to see most clearly in older toddlers as their understanding of language and their thoughts are more advanced than their use of language. In this stage, you will often hear a toddler use noises or alternative words along with gestures or pointing to try to make their meanings clear when they aren't being understood.

 You can further support this move by asking questions such as; "Can you tell me some colours?" or "Can you tell me some animals?" For younger toddlers also provide the examples yourself as you point to the thing you are talking about; "What colours do we know? We know red and blue and green and yellow."

Y – YIELD

Toddlers are not the best candidates for yielding, though they often don't have a choice. They are usually very set in their mind and wants and don't want to yield to adults, their peers, or (often) reality if it doesn't fit with what they want. Have you ever seen a toddler get frustrated because they can't get their foot into a sock or tried to get a toddler into a car seat when they don't want to be put in it? They are not the best yielders. So how can we help to teach this move?

The most common way is when we teach our toddlers things they can and can't do. They can't climb up the bookcase, they can't have chocolate for breakfast, and they do have to go in their car seat. As toddlers grow, they begin to realise that the world doesn't work on their sheer will power, and they do have to yield now and then. You can support this in tiny ways (without major tantrums) by doing things like offering the choice they might not want. For example, giving them the building block that they didn't request or telling them "Toast now, chocolate later". Encouraging them to share when with another child is also a step towards being able to yield.

Z – ZOOM

In Thinking Moves, you can zoom in (see the details) or zoom out (see the bigger picture). The skill most useful with toddlers is to be able to zoom in and look at the details.

Zooming is a skill that is useful for carers of toddlers when toddlers get upset or angry. By zooming in to what the toddler is doing or has just been doing, instead of making assumptions, it will be easier to figure out what the problem is.

You can help your toddler to learn to zoom in by spending a lot of time on each page of a picture book and looking at the details of the illustrations instead of just racing through the story.

Chapter 6 – Philosophical Three to Five-Year-Olds

Ok, things are about to get exciting! You have done three years of leg work, and now your child or children are ready to use the moves all by themselves. Is this step still possible if this is the first time you have ever looked at Thinking Moves? Of course! As you will have already learnt, the majority of the Thinking Moves are so intuitive and natural that you have probably been doing most of them before you even knew they existed anyway. Now that children are age three and older, they begin to combine moves more often as their interactions and thoughts become more complex and multi-layered.

Now into the world that you are probably most familiar with. That of three to five-year-olds. As you will know a lot of growth has happened since these children were born. I always find it amazing how much growth occurs in those first three years. Before I taught pre-schoolers, I always assumed that three-year-olds were pretty much the same the world over. Even as a mother (pre-teaching career), I thought that three-year-olds were pretty similar. Well, I would wouldn't I? So would anyone not working with young children. You might hang out with other kids sometimes, but these kids are probably coming from a similar background and environment to your own. The children are different, but on the grand scale of things, they are much of a muchness.

It is only when you begin to work with young children that you realise that they vary greatly, most importantly, in their communication and language skills. By now, a typically developing child will be talking using simple sentences. Although some children will still be at the stage of three words, most will be beginning to use more complex sentences using words like 'and' and 'because'. They will be starting to understand simple questions and will be asking questions of their own. Most prolifically 'why?' **(QUESTION)**

Most children will now be experts at role play and imaginary play and will have absorbed three to four years of language, stories, television, and song. They will be able to understand emotions when supported, and starting to realise that their own actions can affect other people's feelings.

Children of this age will not necessarily have the best moral judgment themselves, but they do now have a sense of justice, most often knowing when something is 'bad/wrong' or 'good/right' (CONNECT/DIVIDE) and, being the most pressing issue in a young child's life, the concept of fairness (JUSTIFY). This will usually raise its head with both unreasonable requests ('I want a big chocolate bar, not a small one. That's not fair') and those that are more reasonable ('He isn't sharing. It's my turn').

Also, on their personal and social development, they will be starting to be able to imagine themselves in other real-life scenarios **(PICTURE)**. For example, they can imagine then answer the question "How would you feel if you got lost?" which they probably weren't able to do in their toddler years. They can also understand and answer more complex questions more effectively, though the answers may conform to their child logic and not necessarily to the logic of adults.

Three to five-year-olds are at the stage where a philosophical approach is not purely appropriate just within play anymore but can be introduced more formally. As a side note, you may be pulling your hair out and shouting at the page right about now because I keep using the phrase 'typically developing' and who of us ever gets a class made entirely up of typically developing children?

Don't worry; I am using this phrase just to make it clear that the developmental stages I have been talking about are for a typically developing child and not the expectation for every child in your class. As you read on, you will find advice on using Thinking Moves with children who have special educational needs. Most importantly, don't worry about having to include all children in focused sessions. If it causes a child more distress than benefit, then they can still have full access to a philosophical approach to teaching without the need to do focused sessions.

By the age of three to four years old, a typically developing child will be talking using simple sentences. Many children will be using more complex sentences using words like 'and' and 'because' (JUSTIFY). They will be starting to understand simple questions and will be asking questions of their own (QUESTION/RESPOND). Most prolifically 'why?' Most children will now be experts at role play and imaginary play and will have absorbed three to four years of language, stories, television, and song **(BACK)**. They will be able to understand emotions when supported and starting to realise that their own actions can affect other people's feelings.

Philosophical Skill – Listening and Attention

3 to 5-year olds are now at a stage where they can sit for short periods, listen and respond appropriately to questions **(QUESTION/RESPOND)**. Some are more able than others but, with support, most of them are now ready to be able to have 10 to 15-minute focused Philosophy for Children sessions. If you would like to introduce formal Philosophy for Children sessions, then you will find different organisations and approaches to explore towards the end of this book.

It has always seemed a bit of a paradox to me that pre-schoolers seem to stop asking questions once their language skills develop. Where do those 'whys' go? Some children carry on asking questions, but I often find that quite a few stop. Perhaps they get used to generic 'just because' answers, designed to stop them asking. Whatever the reason, now is the perfect time not to let that thirst for knowledge dry up. It is up to us to keep that thirst alive and provide a constant flow of information, questions, and conversation to feed it.

Philosophical Skill – Imagination and Social Skills

It is time for rapid progress in both imagination and social skills. Children understand more about the world and each other. What's more, they have started to show interest in their peers, in their personalities and lives (CONNECT/DIVIDE/LISTEN/LOOK). Their role-play now becomes more complex and imaginative. It is not unusual to see a group of pre-schoolers play an in-depth role-play game with narratives and storylines where they interact and react to what is said by the other friends in play

(LISTEN/LOOK/QUESTION/RESPOND). These games can often be put away, as they flick back to reality for their lunch or snack break, then pulled back out of their imaginary closet as they resume the game exactly where they left off once sent to play again (BACK).

Already showing philosophical enquiry skills as they imagine and act out different scenarios and change their thinking and outcomes according to the involvement of other children or adults (WEIGH UP/VARY). Children begin to understand cause and effect, consequences, and emotions – both of their friends and characters in their play (CONNECT/DIVIDE). They are talented at managing this double life in their minds. They can be playing as superheroes one minute, knowing that this is all with the consent of the other players, yet also know when someone is genuinely hurt, and the 'superhero' turns back into a real friend who needs help (INFER). They know now what is real and what is pretend (CONNECT/DIVIDE). More than once I have gone along with pretend play and, obviously being such an amazing actress (I must have missed my calling) been a bit too convincing leading to a child saying 'it's only pretend' (EXPLAIN).

We can help this philosophical play by knowing when to stand back and observe and when to get involved and role-play ourselves. We can also furnish children with all we know about different characters (EXPLAIN/eXEMPLIFY/HEADLINE) so that they can explore them themselves during play (USE). This may mean carpet time inputs, chat, or stories about every character we can think of from fairytale characters to real-life occupations and different ways of life around the world (PICTURE/EXPLAIN/eXEMPLIFY). We can also make sure a wide range of structured (dress-ups and props) and unstructured (junk modelling, large boxes, bits and bobs) resources are available at all times.

Philosophical Skill – Problem Solving

Our children have been amateur problem solvers since birth. How do I get my carer's attention? How do I get that food to my mouth? How do I get across the floor to my toy? How do I move my legs and arms alternately to crawl, walk, run? How do I get that off the shelf? (QUESTION)

Now at the pre-school level, their problem-solving skills are reaching their first all-time high. The problems they can solve are not just physical and immediate anymore. Oh no. Now they have the skills to listen to imaginary scenarios (PICTURE) and figure out a world of different possible actions and outcomes (WEIGH UP/INFER/PICTURE).

By this stage, children have started to develop an awareness of cause and effect, and it's relative predictability (ORDER/SIZE/TEST) but also the ability to consider other possible outcomes if the first action is changed. Would you always help a friend? Yes. But what if they were doing something that was going to get you in trouble? Oh well, in that case... (WEIGH UP/VARY/MAINTAIN/NEGATE). You can introduce problem-solving into all areas of the classroom. From having specific baskets for specific toys at tidy-up time to having regular mathematics activities to physical challenges like climbing and running games.

Once again, and for the last time, I ask... was there anything you weren't already doing anyway? No? See – you are already a philosophical practitioner or parent.

Formal Sessions

Ages three to five years are also a great time to introduce some more formal 15-minute sessions based around an activity and with a small group of children (though if you are doing this at home, it will also still work with just one child). When working in a group you can even begin to focus on the 4Cs of Philosophy for Children (Collaborative, Critical, Caring and Creative) and get children more used to the semantics of Thinking Moves as they learn the Thinking Move name and the linking sign language action (https://dialogueworks.co.uk/teacher-toolkit/)

When doing Philosophy for Children, I have always used my QUEST model. QUEST is an acronym for Question; Understanding; Exploring; Sharing; Thanks (and Thoughts). I have included a couple of examples in the following pages to show how this can be used for groups or just one child. Since the introduction of Thinking Moves, however, Amanda Hubball has created a great Thinking Moves based alternative for QUEST.

The letters here stand for Question; Use; Explain; Size; Test (I am sure by now, you have become confident enough to have spotted that those are all Thinking Moves).

Chapter 7 – Thinking Moves With Three to Five-Year-Olds

You are probably now becoming a bit of an expert with Thinking Moves yourself, and the children we are dealing with are older. We now enter the exciting time when we can start to combine several moves in just one activity and see how they work symbiotically. I will suggest a few links in the following chapter, but I bet you can find extra moves that link to each activity without my help.

If you are working in an Early Years setting and want specific activities linking to the Early Years Foundation Stage, then please visit *DialogueWorks* (https://dialogueworks.co.uk/) or *Magical Mess of the EYFS* (https://magicalmess.weebly.com/). On both of these websites, you will find lots of lesson plans and Development Matters (UK) links along with other Thinking Moves resources. For more day to day opportunities read on.

A -AHEAD

At ages three to five, we now have great little thinkers who are more than ready for thinking ahead. One way to practice this skill every day is to talk about what is coming up later in the day, tomorrow, or further in the future, such as at the weekend or special events. Keep using and expanding future tense vocabulary but make the words you introduce more future-facing such as 'at the weekend', 'next week', 'next month', 'on your birthday' or 'next year.' You can also combine this move with **PICTURE** as you talk about 'what might happen if...'

Thinking ahead is also a good move when combined with **FORMULATE** and **WEIGH UP** if you ask a child to problem solve or plan an activity before they start it—for example, providing them with various tools and items to transfer water from one place to another and getting them to decide what one item would work best to do the task.

B – BACK

Children have a great memory by this age. More than once have I heard the phrase from a three-year-old "But you said…" then cursed because they have remembered a promise I half-heartedly made several days earlier. In addition to carrying on with the past tense words that you started in the toddler years and the word 'remember', you can now take a more focused approach to think back. Try this by playing This Is Your Life. Ask another adult or child to talk about their day or a memory of their own while your child listens (LISTEN). Afterwards, ask them questions about the story they just heard (QUESTION/RESPOND/BACK).

You can do the same with storybooks by asking questions after you have finished each page or the book. You can also use thinking back when telling a child why they shouldn't do something ("What happened last time you ran indoors?") or to work out what they should do next ("Can you remember last time we made playdough? What did we do wrong to make it too sloppy?") For a great working memory game try Kim's Game. Have a selection of items and cover it with a cloth. Remove one item secretly them remove the fabric. Can your child think back and tell you which item is missing?

C – CONNECT and D – DIVIDE

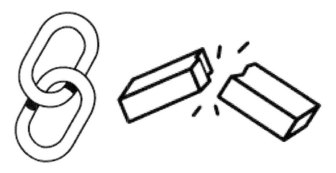

Now experts at these two moves, three to five-year-olds can begin to do them in tandem. A lovely game to use these two moves is Odd One Out. Choose three items that could be said to be all the same but also all different. For example, choose three cars that all have similarities and differences and ask your child or children "Which is the odd one out? Why?" If you choose carefully, this game can go on for a long time.

You may need to model first by explaining "I think this car is the odd one out because it has no red on it. It is divided from the other two cars. The other two cars are connected. They are the same because they both have red on." Then choose a different odd one out and explain why you think this is the odd one out.

You can then move on to either choosing the odd one out yourself and asking your child or children "Why do you think this is the odd one out?". Older children should separate the items themselves and tell you why the one they removed was the odd one out. Use a minimum of three things and a maximum of five.

You will often see connecting and dividing in role-play. Children may divide themselves into baddies and goodies, parents and children or humans and animals. They also display their ability to make connections when they decide to be a character and dress up to look like (and in their eyes become) them.

This is an excellent combination of moves when looking at tolerance and acceptance as you can explore similarities and differences between children and their friends or their families and other families. Children can learn that, despite being different, we are all the same in some very essential ways yet different in others.

Everything we do now helps to create creative and critical thinkers as children get older. This sort of activity opens the door for later learning about the unfairness of prejudice and discrimination and societal or systematic inequalities concerning race, religion, gender, age, belief, disability and sexual orientation.

E – EXPLAIN

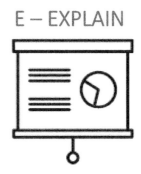

Anyone who has ever asked a three or four-year-old who started a fight or how they hurt their finger will know that explaining clearly is a skill that most children are still learning. The Thinking Move **HEADLINE** is useful for getting to the root of a matter but mastering the craft of explaining helps children to pad out the main headline with relevant details. Children do display this skill often, as they tell you what their barely recognizable drawing is about or try to tell you what they want or think. The way we can best support children as they learn to explain is by shutting up! I am sure I am not the only one who has a default setting of trying to paraphrase or assume I know what a child is saying rather than let them take their time to get all of their words out. Likewise, when a child is mid-tantrum, we will often assume we know the reason for the tantrum and go forth with that assumption. How frustrated children must get with us adults sometimes! The best thing we can all do to support this it to just slow down and say "Explain to me what..." and actually shut our mouths and listen. To take a more focused approach, you could play games where the child needs to explain to you what item to pick up without saying the name of the item or describe to you where something is using positional language. Another fun game is for the child to explain to you an imaginary character and for you to draw it as per their directions.

F – FORMULATE

After a couple of years formulating, from working out how to reach a toy during tummy time to navigating how to get their own way through cuteness or tantrums, three-year-olds are now well versed in the skill of formulating to get their own way.

Now is the time to get them formulating on your agenda instead of theirs. The best way to do this is by setting challenges and problems such as; presenting all of the ingredients needed to make buns but no instructions or setting a challenge to make a robot out of junk modelling. You could set an activity threading a lace through beads and offer jigsaw puzzles with increasing difficulty. The list of puzzles and challenges you can set to practice **FORMULATE** is endless.

G – GROUP

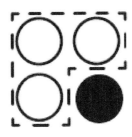

Grouping is yet another skill that gets even more fun now that your child or children are getting more conscious of the world. Three-year-olds can be set tasks to group by colour or by simple characteristics such as soft and hard toys. Older three-year-olds and young four-year-olds can be expected to group by more detailed features, such as different types of animal (farm or zoo), dinosaur (carnivores and herbivores) or produce (comes from an animal or comes from the ground).

 As children get older, begin to group by more abstract concepts such as items that would be useful on an adventure and those that wouldn't. For older four-year-olds and five-year-olds you can also group in a way that encourages teamwork, for example tasking a group of children to sort themselves out into a group who like carrots and a group that doesn't. Once this skill is embedded, you can group by anything. In literacy, you could group by fairy tale characters and Julia Donaldson characters. In mathematics group by odd numbers and even numbers. In understanding the world group by insects that have wings and those without, group the items, you find on a nature walk (leaves, flowers, sticks, stones) or group clothes by season or location. When you begin to teach phonics, group numerals and letters separately to help children to notice and understand which characters are numbers and which are letters.

A useful and visual way to group is by putting items into two separate hoops, for example, one hoop for herbivores and one for carnivores. If something seems to be in both groups and your child or the children cannot come to a decision, then this gives you the flexibility of crossing the hoops in the middle to make a Venn diagram where the items which could go in both groups end up in the middle section. In this example, you would end up with omnivores in the crossed middle section. There are so many possibilities with this move that **GROUP** is the gift that keeps on giving, and it partners very well with many of the other Thinking Moves.

H – HEADLINE

Headlining is a skill that benefits children in their everyday lives and academically. Getting children into a habit of being able to give you the headline can improve communication and reduce frustration no end. This is a classic example of a Thinking Move for which teaching the word will be easy once you get going.

Next time a child wants you to do something or is in the middle of a drama and trying to explain (but not doing very well) say to them "Give me the headline" then help them with who/what/where/when/why/how questions.

As you do this more regularly, you will no longer need the questions as the child will understand precisely what "Give me the headline" means. You can also practice this skill by simplifying stories.

Read the page of a picture book and then ask "What is the headline?" For example, if you read out "Once upon a time, there was a little girl who lived with her mother in a beautiful forest. She always smiled, and her name was Red Riding Hood because of the lovely red cape that she wore."

Work with your child or children to 'find the headline' by cutting out all of the words until you are left with the important ones... "A little girl called Red Riding Hood lived with her mother in the woods. She had a red cape" (or even shorter).

I – INFER

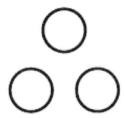

Inference is a skill that will come quickly to some children but will be very difficult for others, especially children who may take things too literally.

One activity you could do is to look at children in different situations and with various emotions such as a picture of a child laughing at a fairground or a picture of a child crying in a park. Can the children tell you how that child is feeling? How do they know? Why do they think they are feeling that way? What clues can they see in the picture?

Having a bag or basket of clues for a story can be an enjoyable activity starter too. If you have a basket with three bowls in three different sizes and a bag of porridge, can your child guess what story you will be reading today?

Another activity could be playing "What could that mean?" You can do this with any theme and give clues so that your child can practice inferring. The clues could be as simple as dipping your finger in some water and saying 'ouch' or shivering. Can your child infer what either of these responses means about the temperature of the water? You could have more complex games of "What could that mean?", for example by having a selection of clothes and choosing just some to put on (swimming goggles and flippers – what could that mean?) or packing different items in a suitcase and asking "Where would we be going if we packed this type of clothing?"

J – JUSTIFY

Justify is a close relative of INFER and for all of your inference games, you can then ask for a child to justify why they made that assumption/inference. A great way to get a child to justify is to turn the tables on them. Remember when they used to ask you 'why?' all the time? Time to get revenge. When you are having conversations about books, cartoons, or any part of the world you see during the day as them 'why?' in as many different situations as you can.

If you want to start the conversation off, then ask "Why do you think…?" or act as if you don't know something and see if you can get their help… "I was wondering. Why is the sky blue? Why do you think the sky is blue?" When your child asks you a why question turn that question back around and ask them why as you get closer to the truth of the pondering together.

K – KEYWORD

Finding the keyword can be easier or harder than finding the **HEADLINE** depending on the child or situation. It is often easier to tackle keywords first, though, and then build them into a headline. Imagine a child coming to you in tears and giving a long, rambling, confusing tale about how they got hurt. A story that involves five children, three different areas of the park, and a squirrel can really be pulled down to the keywords "John/pushed/slide" and then build back to the headline "We were all playing, and John pushed me to get on the slide".

Just like getting children to learn to "Give me the headline" it can help to teach them to "Give me the keywords". From your point of view, it might be a case of narrowing down the keywords for the child. "What are our keywords? Did you hurt yourself on the swing or the slide? Jill or John? Did the squirrel do anything?" Keyword games are also great fun. It is a lovely way to remember or recap any story or any learning as you make a mind map. You might make a mind map with all of the keywords from The Three Little Pigs or one with all of the keywords your child remembers from the learning you did about the life cycle of a butterfly or seed.

L – LISTEN/LOOK

Most children have now been listening or looking for three or more years by now. They are now capable of being more proactive listeners and lookers instead of passive. The key to being an active listener or looker is not just to take in the necessary information but also to take on finer details and respond appropriately.

The most natural way to do this is to practice having conversations with your child. Sure they can tell you all about things and answer questions based on their interests but can they listen to the things that you say that are based on your interests and ask you questions or do they get bored and bring the conversation back to themselves? A proactive listener is one who sincerely engages in the conversation.

As well as conversations, there are various games you can play to build these skills. Great books to look at together are Nick Sharratt's *You Choose* books (Pippa Goodhart and Nick Sharratt, *You Choose* [Puffin, 2018]), which have many small details on each page. Looking at all of the pictures and having two-way conversations about what you see and think will help to build the skill of looking and listening.

Much like you did in the toddler years now is an excellent time to talk about the difference between seeing and hearing. You can't hear "a bird in a tree". You hear a bird, but you don't know that it is in a tree unless you see it there. You can't hear a "big dog barking". You can **INFER** it from the sound, but you have to look to see what size it is. You can hear the wind, but you can't see it. Look around for visual clues that the wind is blowing. Now is a great time to start to go on minibeast hunts too.

Another listening game to play is hide and seek. You (or another child) hide with a bell and ring it for a second. Can your child follow the sound to find you? For looking (and in combination with **GROUP**) go on a shape hunt. How many triangular things can you find? How many circular things? Or a number or letter hunt. Ages three to five are the times to turn these passive skills into more focused and proactive skills.

It is worth noting, that at this age **LISTEN/LOOK** also means to be able to look inside of yourself and listen to your feelings and thoughts so it can be used as a method of exploring and regulating emotions.

M – MAINTAIN

Now that your children are more aware of their own opinions and that other people might have different views, it is time to explore maintaining on a deeper level. In a group, this can be done by voting on an issue ("Which makes the best pet – a cat or a dog?") then arguing their case. On a one-to-one basis, you could have a similar dialogue as you discuss an issue. Does your child maintain their own opinion, at least for a little while? During play, you may see children of this age, maintaining their point of view as they stick to their approach rather than copying others. You will also hear children maintaining their beliefs or opinions or views in arguments with their peers. You could get children used to making their own minds up about their beliefs by playing a Yes/No game as you ask questions (Are all cats furry? Are all fairies good? Is ice cream better than cake?) and get all children to say 'yes' or 'no'. If you team this up with **JUSTIFY,** then you can get even more out of the game.

N – NEGATE

Now out of the stage of saying 'no' just to drive us crazy, three-year-olds and older say no to disagree with people for more logical and in-depth reasons than merely wanting their own way. Despite us sometime wanting younger children to say 'no' a little bit less, it does have several benefits. Though technically the opposite of maintaining, negating does give children a tool to be able to say no to others when being tempted into doing the wrong thing. Being able to negate and maintain are two sides of the same coin – that of being an individual with independent thought. A positive way to play with negating is to be a saboteur when formulating plans. For example, we can return to the playdough making. Yes again (isn't playdough great?). Have all of the ingredients ready for a child to experiment with. Ask how we make playdough. Then pose some what-ifs – what if we only have half as much water/no salt/ no spoon? Each time you negate an idea, your child will have to think of a new approach to negate your negation! Try it out by talking about what to do tomorrow. "What should we do tomorrow?" "Go to the park" "But what if it rains?" "We could wear our wellington boots" "But what if there is a hole in one of our boots?" and so on. The skill of negating can make for some great creative and critical thinking.

O – ORDER

Ordering is much easier for three to five-year-olds than it was for toddlers. Now more adept at **LISTEN/LOOK** and **GROUP**, children can begin to put things in a logical order. This can be ordering by properties (size, length, weight, height, etc.) or opinion (like the most/least, would be most useful/least useful, etc.). Children are now able to order more than three things (though don't go over the top as you will find they often get bored if working with more than six or seven items). It is an excellent time to introduce a concept continuum. The easiest way to do this is by either drawing a line on the floor with a piece of chalk or putting a rope on the floor. You can then label each end however you wish; best/worst, like most/like least, most scary/least scary, etc. You can then chat and decide which order to put the items on along the line. Ordering can also be read as 'sequencing'. You can get many sequencing games and cards from online shops or make them yourself. Cards could be as straightforward or as complicated as you think is needed for the child. A younger child might work on sequencing the events of a birthday party (picture of a child receiving a gift > picture of the child opening gift> picture of the child smiling with toy> picture of the child playing with the toy). In contrast, an older child might be able to use picture cards to sequence a whole fairy tale that they have listened to. Sequencing for some children may be as simple as now and next (now we are going to do some reading > next we will play out).

P – PICTURE

Picturing is a Thinking Move that works well alongside several other Thinking Moves. Picturing can mean thinking of something in your mind then explaining it to someone else (EXPLAIN). It could mean picturing yourself in a particular situation or how you or someone else may feel, recalling a memory and picturing that event in your head (BACK), or imagining something which could happen in the future (AHEAD).

Once a child reaches three years old, they become more adept at all of these skills, some with a little bit of support needed. Ask your child to picture a birthday party and tell you about it. Ask questions to push for future details. Who will be there? What food will there be? What games will they play? To make it a more straightforward task, ask a child to describe an object.

Get them to picture a house or a car or a cow and describe it to you. Another way of picturing in everyday life is to encourage your child to imagine how they might feel in somebody else's situation. For example "George is new in class today. How do you think he might feel?" or "How would you feel if somebody snatched your toy?"

This could be extended to story characters too. How do you think Baby Bear felt when he realised his porridge was gone and his chair was broken?

You could also talk about sensory input and imagine that. What do you think clouds feel like? What do you think it would feel like to sit in a bath of jelly? What do you think rabbit fur feels like?

A great active game you can play is to get your child to tell you what character they would like to be, then send them off to find all of the resources they need to make a fancy dress costume to become that character. Make sure there are no character-specific items around and instead have a variety of other items so that your child has to picture what the character would look like them use their imagination to create the character from the resources available **(FORMULATE/VARY)**.

Q – QUESTION

The ability to question is one which comes naturally to some children, but many children will need support to understand how to do this. I regularly ask my class of three and four-year-olds if they have any questions (either for me, for a friend, or about a story or topic) and the majority will struggle to understand the difference between asking a question and giving an answer.

I try to build this knowledge by saying phrases such as "oh, you have a question" or "that is a good question" whenever a child asks a question during the day. In a focused session, I will say "well done for asking a question" and will use the corresponding sign language for QUESTION (a question mark drawn in the air with my finger). If what they have given me is information I will say "that isn't a question but thank you for telling me about that/that information/explaining that to me".

If it seems useful and relevant, I will use the sign language for EXPLAIN (two hands moving one at once from your chin outwards).

If possible, I will also say "I will ask you a question" and ask a question about what the child just said. The primary key to this skill is to teach children the difference between questions and information through modelling and games. The sign language for Thinking Moves can be found on the DialogueWorks website. All of the signs are based on the British Sign Language for the actual word or one of its synonyms.

One game you could play is the "What Is It?" game. For this, you need an item of curiosity – something none of the children will have ever seen. The children need to ask you questions to figure out what the item is. Another game could be to have a selection of cups and tubs in different colours and hide a toy under one then encourage your child to ask questions to find out where the toy is. A useful skill for yourself is to get used to using the phrase "I have a question..." before you ask a question.

R – RESPOND

Most three to five-year-olds can respond when asked a question, but can they respond appropriately? By age five then they usually can, but for three and four-year-olds it can sometimes be trickier; even more so if it is a child who has fixed interests or chooses not to listen when something does not interest them.

We can, and usually do, plan around child interests and this does help to teach the basics of responding, however, to excel at this move, children need to be able to respond and share their ideas, opinion, or thoughts when the topic is not one of their choosing.

One way to get children to be better responders is something which we all think we do, but we can probably all do better. That is to show genuine interest in each child's ideas and opinions. It can be easy, as a carer or educator, to slip into the habit of asking questions and being focused on needing a specific answer. It is this that often shuts children off from responding. Children are very quick at realising when we don't genuinely care about their thoughts or ideas and quick to shut off when they realise they aren't giving us the answer we are looking for.

Luckily most children between the ages of three and five are still impulsive enough to give responses without needing to know their response will be the 'right' one. It is at those times that we need to show that we value any contribution the child has made and are interested in their thoughts. Aim to have dialogues with children that last for at least ten back and forth interactions.

If you are in a larger setting (as opposed to reading this as a parent or childminder), then get into the habit of thanking reluctant responders when they do choose to get involved in a conversation. If you feel it would embarrass them in front of their peers then just a quick sentence later in the day, "I liked your answer to my question/Well done for being brave and joining in/I really enjoyed hearing what you thought about..." will work just as well, if not better.

Quick games of Would You Rather? or Do You Prefer? will also get less confident children more comfortable with responding as their answers are limited to two choices which you have given them and based on their own opinion so guaranteed not to be wrong.

S – SIZE

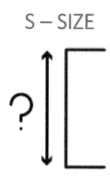

At age three to five sizing becomes more of a complicated task. It can mean figuring out the exact size, weight, amount, or space of time or can be more about estimating. A good prerequisite for sizing is being able to count accurately and being able to subitize (accurately estimate). To gain this skill children need to have at least a vague knowledge that ten is more than five, twenty is a 'big' number, one hundred is a lot, and one thousand is probably more than they can imagine. For some children, this skill comes more easily than counting accurately. It is worth noting here that the skill of estimating and understanding language relating to quantity is just as important for children as it is for adults. One of the first things you can work on is attributing some meaning to words of quantity, for example, what is the difference to you, and the children, between 'all', 'most', 'many' and 'lots'?

You can help them to learn how to estimate and count at the same time by holding up fingers or putting down objects and asking them to guess how many. Once they have guessed you say "Let's count to find out". Make sure you take a (slightly wrong) guess yourself after the child has done their estimation and talk it through as you do it to add an extra layer of number sense. "I can see there are a few, so there are more than one, but there aren't lots and lots, so it is less than twenty. Not one hundred because that is a huge number. I am guessing that there are seven apples." As an aside, the skill of estimating is an essential one for

Philosophy for Children. Not because philosophers need to be amazing at maths, but because it instils a mindset in children that they are allowed to give answers that might be 'wrong'. This gives them a level of bravery that is sometimes needed to put their thoughts and opinions out there in front of their peers.

Sizing can also be done with time games. Set up a one-minute egg timer and see if children can close their eyes and guess when the minute is up. Ask how long the children think it will take to tidy the toys up and set a timer for that amount of time (there are many timers on YouTube which you can set running on a whiteboard or TV so that the children can see). If you are baking, get the children to estimate how long they think you should leave the cake in the oven. Talk them through what would happen if you left it for two hours and what would happen if you left it for two minutes.

This is a great time to introduce words such as second, minute, hour, day, week, etc. It is a good step in the right direction to begin to estimate how much food it takes to fill you up too. Ask your child to let you know how much food they might need for their meal and begin to talk about how much we need to eat and why along with what is too much. As you can see, SIZE is a far more extensive and varied Thinking Move than you would assume from the name.

T – TEST

As they have learnt to test out many things by now, from foods to crawling and walking, to their skills and abilities, children at age three are now ready to make a metacognition leap and start to test their ideas and beliefs.

Working well alongside **FORMULATE** and **USE**, testing is an essential step in a lot of what we do as we learn.

TEST is a word that children can quite quickly begin to understand and use. As we have taught them to 'test' the temperature of their food before they put it in their mouth and similar everyday uses of the word, we can now begin to introduce it as a useful step in working things out for themselves.

One way to do this is to ask for ideas about how to do something in real life, ("How can we drop this egg without breaking it?) then try the ideas out ("Drop it onto a cushion? Let's test that idea.").

Another would be to work on creative thinking about hypotheticals ("Some people don't believe in fairies but you do. How could we test if fairies exist? How many ideas can you think of").

You can also set challenges. First, get children to **FORMULATE** plans ("What would be the quickest way to get our toy dinosaur out of this big block of ice?) then **TEST** out all of the different ideas.

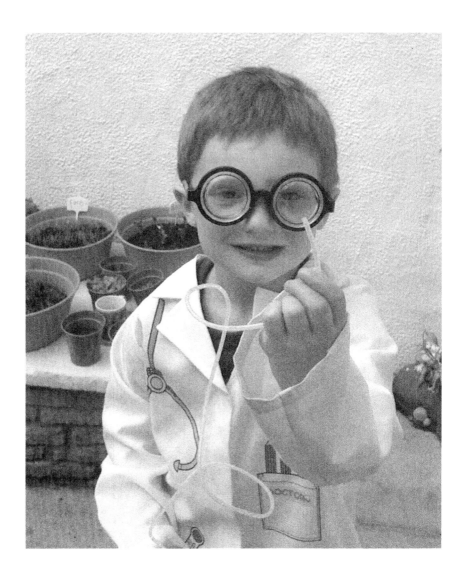

U – USE

By now, children have built up a whole stock of knowledge, and we teach them more every day. A great habit to get into is using the phrase "Let's use what we know." It covers a whole host of situations. "How can we cool the water down? Let's use what we know about hot and cold.", "What could we do to cheer her up? Let's use what we know about her." "How could we spell the word 'wish'? Let's break it down and use what we know."

You can also use this move for particularly emotional children who struggle to calm down when they are upset or angry. Once you have given them some tools for self-regulation then you can remind them that they have those tools to use whenever they need, "I can see you are really angry, let's use our blowing up a balloon game to calm down. Take a deep breath and pretend to blow up an invisible balloon..."

In a more concrete sense of the word you could play games that focus on the use of objects, for example how many uses your child can think of for a shell or showing your child an apron and seeing how many people and tasks you can think of where an apron would be used. Both of these games can also cover the Thinking Move of **VARY**.

V – VARY

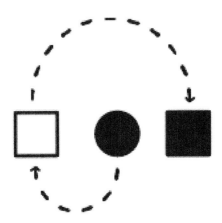

To vary something is to alter or change it. Children have already done a lot of this by the age of three as they have learnt to navigate the world. They have tried one way to reach a toy, and it hasn't worked, so they try a different way. Without the ability to vary their approach, they would never have learnt to crawl, walk, or talk. The ability to vary is at the very route of building resilience – we get knocked down, but we get back up again.

As natural users of variation, this is a move that children are now at a stage to begin to do more purposefully, as they can now deal with more setbacks and bounce back from them (no longer a slave to their toddler's it's not fair' emotions). A great game from the Thinking Moves book (which feeds in well to literacy in the Early Years) is 'New Choice!' Though this game is for slightly older children, it can be varied (see what I did there?) to be age-appropriate for younger children.

For this game take a story that your child already knows and change one detail every page. "Once upon a time, there were three little pigs." "Should we change the word 'little' or the word 'pigs'? What should we change it to?"

Another game that we call "But what if...?" (which also appears in Thinking Moves as 'Socrates' Sieve') lets you have a prolonged dialogue to encourage variation of thoughts. To do this, you pose a seemingly simple question and then take a 'but why?' approach to responding to whatever your child says. For example: 'Should we always help our friends? But what if they are doing something wrong?' This can also be used for safety talks: 'Should we ever talk to grown-ups we don't know? But what if you get lost and need help?' It is also a great way to explore past behaviour: 'What did you do when you got angry at Tim? What could you have done differently?' You will find that varying is also a great tool when trying any task that might not work the first time and may need a different approach. It is a great motivator never to give up.

W – WEIGH UP

Weighing things up gives us a metacognition tool that helps us to make decisions, hopefully, the right choices. It means taking all of the evidence to hand, including our own opinions and past experiences, to make an active choice. It is a skill that does not always come naturally to our more impulsive children but, once taught, can be an excellent tool for children to avoid a world of problems as they grow up.

We already support our children with this as we ask "What do you think?" "What do you want to do?" "What should you have done?" "Which one would you like?" Now is the time when we can teach children to begin to make more of a conscious effort to weigh up things.

You could do this in a practical sense by getting them to weigh up different approaches to tasks such as building or navigating an assault course or play area. Children can also make choices such as which cartoon character they would like to invite for a tea party or which of two activities to do later that day. When weighing up options we usually talk about pros and cons but for this age it is better to talk about 'good things about...' and 'bad things about...'

X – eXEMPLIFY

As children's vocabulary increases, so do their abilities to give examples for things. These examples can also begin to extend into more conceptual areas. Now is the time to push your children beyond simple examples ("Can you tell me some examples of farm animals?") and towards more complex ones ("Can you give me examples of things that might make you upset?"). You can also begin to get children used to giving examples when you do not understand what they are trying to explain ("You want to play a game? Can you give me an example of the type of game you would like to play?").

You can use this move to test further understanding ("How many examples of sea creatures can you think of? Should we find some more examples?"). At this age, when children are beginning to either conform to or struggle with rules, it can also be a nice way to give positive reinforcement ("That was so helpful Ali. What a good example you are setting.").

Y – YIELD

As children get older, they become more able to listen to the opinion of others and sometimes change their own as a result. Being able to yield (as opposed to always needing to be right) enables us to be better at everything, from learning to relationships. One way to do this is to explore beliefs.

I had two little boys in my class once who were the best of friends, but one of them believed in Santa, and the other didn't. Neither of them could accept that the other one could possibly really believe the opposite to them. They both kept trying to explain to each other in different words why they were right, thinking that maybe their friend just didn't understand what they were talking about. It got to the point of breaking the friendship, and that was when I stepped in with an in the moment Philosophy for Children session on belief.

I got the class to vote with their feet on what they believed in. Go to this side of the room if you believe in unicorns and that side if you don't, go to this side if you believe in dinosaurs and that side if you don't. For this session, I didn't ask anyone to **JUSTIFY** their beliefs; we just kept playing for about ten minutes. By the end of it, the boys still held opposing opinions, but they were both able to yield to the fact that everyone believes different things and that is ok. After that they went on being the best of friends and Santa was never mentioned again. Yielding can be that simple at this age – the acceptance that we are allowed to have different opinions.

Yielding can also be used when teaching children, during play, how to negotiate without conflict. Anyone who has ever worked in Early Years will know this is a daily occurrence. To introduce this as a Thinking Move then you just need to add the word into your conversation whenever a conflict has been resolved ("Well done for giving Lucy a turn. That was great yielding.") and soon children will gain a basic understanding of what the word means. As with all of the moves though, at this age, we are trying to get the children used to the skill, and the name will follow, so don't worry if using the word 'yield' in daily conversation does not feel natural to you.

Z – ZOOM

Zooming in and out is a brilliant tool for any area you would like to learn about with children. Zooming in allows you to look at the details and zooming out enables you to look at the bigger picture.

A good zooming in game is looking at a painting and choosing an area of the painting to look at and talk about. Once you have done this, you can zoom in further to talk about a smaller part of the picture or a character in the picture. Zooming out can also be used in this way when looking at picture books with lots of detail. Children will initially focus on the subject matter which links directly to the words you have said, but can they zoom out and take in the whole picture? Can they then zoom in on a different character and talk about what they might be thinking?

When a child is upset, seemingly about lots of things, it can help to zoom in to get to the root of the problem. This is particularly useful when trying to figure out what has caused an argument or when trying to deal with separation anxiety (What are they really worried about? That mummy won't come back? That they forgot their last kiss? That they don't know where the toilets are or don't know anyone's name?). Zooming in can help us to work out why something we did didn't work (Why did my collage not stick properly?).

Zooming out can be used to look at topics (You live in your house, in your town, in your country, on your continent, in the world, in the galaxy – let's zoom in on another planet). Zoom in to create a child-led topic. If the children want to learn about sea creatures, zoom in and chose a climate, zoom further and choose an animal, zoom further and choose what they want to know about that animal.

Using the phrases **ZOOM IN** and **ZOOM OUT** will become a good habit for any adult dealing with children and can be easily understood by children, especially when the sign language is used too.

As you will have seen Thinking Moves is a brilliant approach for all ages, from birth to adulthood. Sorcha Cowin has been using Thinking Moves with children in Key Stage 1 and has found it an amazing approach to teaching before, during and after the COVID19 lockdown and school closures.

Case Study: Using Thinking Moves in Key Stage 1 (Years 1 and 2) by Sorcha Cowin

In the last academic year, I have been amazed and delighted at how confidently and enthusiastically my class have embraced Thinking Moves and at how well it has worked across all of the school. We have fortnightly assemblies in which I introduce a pair of Thinking Moves icons and synonyms to the whole school and ideas and activities for each type of thinking are explored in more detail in each class before the next TM assembly.

So, how did my Thinking Moves journey begin? During May 2019, I had no idea that a small black book would have such a profound impact on my thinking and teaching. It did not happen straight away. In fact, I am rather embarrassed now with how initially cynical and dismissive I was when I was first skimmed through 'Thinking Moves A-Z: Metacognition Made Simple' especially when we were already focusing on developing metacognitive strategies across the school.

Little did I know that only weeks later, after attending a course and starting to use the moves with Reception class and Year 1 children, I would enthusiastically volunteer to become a facilitator ready to train other people in how to use Thinking Moves in the classroom. I was particularly interested in this due to my experience of leading Philosophy for Children (P4C), an enquiry-based approach to learning and I had seen the direct impact that P4C has on thinking skills. In my teaching, I actively encourage and support children in asking relevant and challenging questions. I believe that this accelerates their ability to think and communicate well, to be better learners. I believed that Thinking Moves would provide learners with the vocabulary that they needed to fully understand and articulate their ideas and the process and progress involved in learning.

My first experience of using the moves in Early Years was for the 'Great Thinking Moves A-Z challenge' just before the summer holidays for each class across the island to try to memorise all of the 26 moves. I was definitely not expecting the 4 and 5-year-olds in my Reception Class to confidently identify all of the icons by naming them accurately when working in groups. In less than ten minutes after sharing the icons and explaining them, they could do this. This seemed too easy. Could it really be so simple to start to introduce the images and vocabulary? Of course, we would need to build on this to achieve a deeper understanding, but they started to talk about the moves and what they thought that they meant straight away. They wanted to use the vocabulary to show how much they understood. Young children are amazing at learning; they instinctively seek challenge and enthusiastically connect ideas, inspiring each other to share their ideas, ask questions and learn from each other.

In September 2019, I moved with my class to teach them in Key Stage 2 as a mixed class of 29 Year 1 and 2 children. I was very excited by how I could continue to use Thinking Moves, and this was a priority area on our School Improvement and Development Plan. During the holidays, I was inspired by the DialogueWorks 'Thinking Moves A-Z Early Years Synonyms' to create the document 'Thinking Moves A-Z with finger spelling' so that the icons, EYFS vocabulary and the BSL alphabet could be easily displayed in our learning environment so that adults and children had visual prompts as we embedded Thinking Moves.

I was so excited to be able to continue to use the 26 moves with the same children, and I envisioned that we would more than likely focus on using a selection of core moves well rather than attempting to actually use all of them. That was the plan. The plan changed. I did not predict that 5 and 6-year-old children would become as proficient in discussing their own thinking using the A-Z vocabulary and be so able to actively reflect on which of the different types of thinking and strategies that they used as quickly as they were able to do so. As the year progressed, we moved to use BSL moves that Sian Greenwood produced with DialogueWorks once they were launched and it was humbling to see how quickly the children could actively use them.

As already mentioned, the timeline that we had envisaged a school was introducing two moves every two weeks. This worked really well for the first half term. Then something amazing happened. We continued to focus on paired moves in detail as planned, but in my classroom, I felt like we became totally immersed in them, and we were ready to do more. It felt absolutely right, and the children naturally started to use the display to suggest other thinking moves that we had not yet focused on in detail. Why? I think that the synonyms explained each type of thinking in a way that just made sense to young children, and I am sure this was the major catalyst for TM being so incredibly successful in my setting. It appeared to be instinctive how they used them. Of course, they had already been using these moves before they ever knew what they were. Thinking Moves are types of thinking, and children are always thinking. Now, however, they just had the right words to identify each type of thinking and explain them easily. Sian's actions also really helped. They were a great way for children to prompt each other too or share their ideas non-verbally.

In each lesson, we talked about our lesson objective and then as a class, decided our steps to success. We framed these with the thinking moves that we used. In the beginning, I carefully guided the children in how to do this. They started to become more and more confident doing this themselves over the first half term and then in the rest of the autumn term; they started to do this for moves that we had not actively focused on yet. Thinking Moves quickly snowballed. It thrived. I felt like we were buzzing with excitement and enthusiasm in lessons. I wish I had better words to describe this atmosphere. It felt like learning was the best thing that we could ever do, and we couldn't get enough of it. It did change the timings of lessons. We spent a lot of time talking about the moves as the children were so engaged by this and keen to explore them further.

In late November, some of the Year 2 children started confidently proposing different moves in lessons and were able to maintain, negate and yield their ideas as they explained their thinking and justified their reasons. Year 1 children started to actively do this in lessons too. It was amazing to experience this. It is important to note that these children were already very experienced in participating in Philosophy for Children (P4C) enquiries or our 'Big Thinking' as we referred to it and they easily transferred and applied these skills in lessons. In my previous school, I had a leadership role for attended P4C, and I had facilitated weekly enquiries for many years. During the academic year 2019-2020, I was also participating in an Early Years P4C and Thinking Moves practice-sharing project between schools in the UK and China. I felt very honored to have been asked to do this, and I have to confess that at times, I felt like an imposter compared to the other very-qualified and inspirational practitioners.

In early December, one of the children in Year 1 spontaneously asked if she could draw the Thinking Moves on her work that she used in her writing after she had received verbal feedback on her work. Of course, I said yes. I was very interested to see how she would do this, and she then asked if she could show the rest of the class too. As she was sharing this with her peers, we had a visitor arrive in our classroom. I knew Nick Chandley from DialogueWorks well, but my class had not met him before. I felt immensely proud that this five-year-old child confidently continued reflecting on her learning in front of a visitor that she did not yet know and could so eloquently share her thinking.

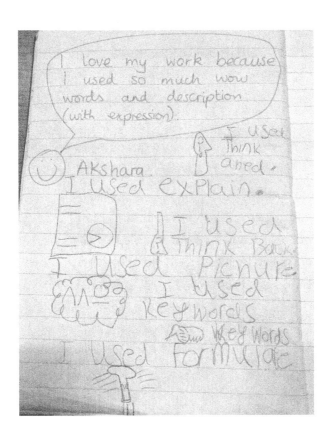

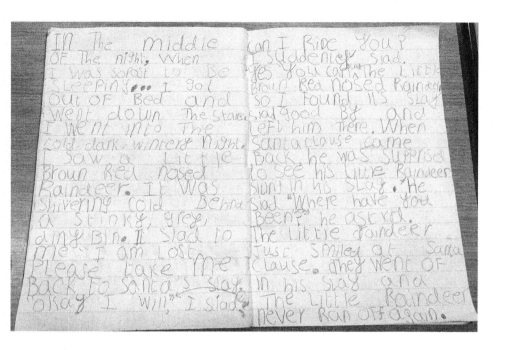

In The middle
OF The night, when
I was so fast to Be
Sleeping... I got
out of Bed and
went down The stairs.
I went into The
cold dark, winters night.
I saw a little
Brown Red nosed
Raindeer. It was
Shivering cold Behind
a stinky, grey,
dirty Bin. I said to
me - I am Lost me.
Please take me
Back To Santa's slay.
"okay I will" I said.

Can I Ride you?
I suddenley said.
Yes you can. The Little
Brown Red nosed Raindeer
so I found his slay
good By and
Left him There. When
Santaclause came
Back, he was supprised
to see his little Raindeer
siun in his slay. He
said "where have you
Been?" he asked.
The Little raindeer
Just smiled at Santa
Clause. They went of
in his slay and
The Little Raindeer
never Ran off again.

Later that day, the other children started to draw and write the moves that they used on their work too. They initiated it. They wanted to do it, so I let them. It was never an expectation that they had to do this even though it was always something that we reflected on verbally in lessons or used strategies like 'thumbs up/thumbs down' or 'vote with your feet' to share our feelings and ideas.

Over the next few months, we became more and more confident discussing our thinking using the language of Thinking Moves. Our P4C discussions became more and more focused and in-depth, and I was consistently amazed by what the children shared with each other without worrying about others' opinions of them. They knew our classroom was a safe space and that ideas could be challenged, nurtured and changed. They started to understand that they could disagree with an idea rather than with a person. During the teaching of inference and deduction in literacy, I was amazed by their ability to formulate ideas by spotting clues in the text and then give reasons for their answers. They maintained, negated and yielded according to what they actually thought rather than being directly influenced by their friend's choices or votes. I was so proud of these 5, 6 and 7-year-olds and their ability to respond to and question ideas. We were using all of the Thinking Moves with so much confidence.

During March 2020, classroom learning changed on the Isle of Man due to the Covid-19 pandemic. Lockdown happened across the island once there were confirmed cases on the island, and we moved to online learning. Hub schools were also open for childcare for parents who were key workers and who did not have the option of children being at home.

On the Isle of Man, schools reopened to all pupils on 22nd June 2020. The island at that stage had no active cases of Covid-19 and social distancing was no longer a requirement. During the lockdown, I had been in contact with all of the children in my class and their parents, both by phoning them, through ItsLearning- our teaching and learning platform, and by teaching many of the children in my class at the Hub school.

I was amazed by how resilient and ready to learn the children were when we physically returned to school. I had anticipated it feeling very different and it being similar to starting the academic year with a new class in September. It wasn't. It was just like we had never had a lockdown. There were times when it felt like the months that we had spent learning at home or at the Hub was something that I made up in my own head because these children came back as if they had never been away from school. I feel very privileged to have been able to experience this and to return to teaching my class in our own classroom to continue our Thinking Moves adventures.

I feel like Thinking Moves has invigorated me as a learner and as a teacher and that it enabled me to better explain my thinking and define it. I am incredibly thankful that I can use it with the learners in my classroom to enable them to do this as well. I have been so lucky to witness so many eureka moments when each of the children in my class naturally realized that they were using actually using a specific thinking move and they named it or signed it-at the start of the year when one child realised that the 'found' socks were actually hers because she used 'Think Back' and could remember seeing them in her PE bag when she was getting changed. She was so excited telling her peers 'I thinked back, I thinked back', and the whole class celebrated this moment with her. Thinking Moves has been so much more than academic learning for my class; they have helped my class in so many ways. In January, one child starting crying at the start of the school day because she was very worried about a family member that was travelling to Australia and she had heard about the devastating bushfires occurring there. We used Zoom in/ Zoom out, Think Back and Think Ahead, Picture and Size to help her to manage her thinking, and I watched this child's anxiety lessen in seconds. It felt natural to use the moves in this way, and it works incredibly well.

I feel like I have gotten to know each child my class so much more by using Thinking Moves, and I am genuinely excited about continuing to use it to demonstrate different thinking strategies and motivate learners. I really believe that they have benefitted each and every individual in my class, including myself. Thinking Moves has changed me. It seems almost incomprehensible that it has only been just over a year since I first discovered such an easy to use and yet incredibly comprehensive way to think about thinking and talk about this with others. It gave me the right words to use and enabled me to easily identify the strategies that we used. I no longer felt like I was wrestling with metacognition. When I think back, I remember struggling for ways to better explain and demonstrate how I was developing metacognitive knowledge and skills in learners.

Metacognition had seemed so difficult to talk about then, even though I knew that I had learned so much about it, and now, now it just makes sense. I am no longer grappling for words. In the past year, I have so often remarked that I wish we had discovered Thinking Moves first. Metacognition really was made simple through these 26 moves.

Chapter 8 – Going On QUESTS

It is all very well saying that Thinking Moves are in everything we do but what if you are the sort of person who likes a more planned approach? It is a common denominator of most Early Years educators that we love a good plan. There is nothing wrong with that. Plans, much like newly bought notebooks, are one of those things that we are sure will solve all of our problems and make us into well oiled educating machines. I love a good plan.

Having a plan does not take away flexibility or a child-led approach. It just gives you a framework and the confidence to know what you want to achieve so that, when you do go off on a tangent or decide to play it by ear, you can do so confidently. It is much like making a plan of how to get from one end of a city to the other in the fastest time but enjoying the odd detour along the way.

You will see in Amanda Hubball's case study, later in this book, her mathematics QUEST model and an example of how it can be used. I encourage you to use this for any of your maths planning if you would like to take a philosophical approach to understand mathematics concepts. I would say it is the perfect way to plan mathematics activities for the Early Years to resist any frameworks or accidental slips into rote learning, as opposed to really understanding the concepts of early maths.

What follows is my P4C QUEST model which is not explicitly Thinking Moves based but can be used comfortably with the moves when the activity you are doing will not fit into the Hubball QUEST model. Between the two models, you will be able to plan any Thinking Moves activity.

In a Hubball QUEST, the letters are linked to Thinking Moves and stand for; Question, Use, Explain, Size, Test. Once you read Amanda's case study, you will see that the Hubball QUEST can be used for mathematics and problem solving but is also transferable to other activities. It also has the benefit of combining five different moves which then work together.

In a Norton-Morris QUEST, the letters stand for; Question, Understanding, Exploring, Sharing, Thanks. This model is more of a generic planning format that can be used for any activity, either individual or group-based. It can also be used for a planned Philosophy for Children session.

Don Quixote by Pablo Picasso (1955)

QUEST Example: A Baby Quest

Baby Quest – A Listening Walk	
Unlike many activities, a listening walk is something you can do from birth. You can go on a walk to the park, into town or even just around your house. This would also work just sitting in the window having a cuddle with the window open to let in extra sounds. An added bonus: try it at bedtime when baby gets older to help them to settle. Unlike plans for toddlers and older children it is best to just focus in on one Thinking Move for babies, even of there are actually several Thinking Moves you use.	
Question	What can we see and hear today? **LOOK/LISTEN**
Understanding	Explain to baby "We are going to go on a listening walk to find out what we can see and hear."
Exploring	Move slowly and take your time. Share lots of eye-to-eye contact to keep baby connected. Whenever you want to point something out say "Look.. it's a..." and point to the thing. Hold baby's face check to cheek with yours to direct their attention. Whenever you want to focus on a noise say "Listen. I can hear a …" Tap your own ear and touch baby's ear. Keep your face and voice expressive.
Sharing	Once you have finished your looking and listening walk, practice these skills further by putting baby in a close up face-to-face position or cradled in your arms and sing some nursery rhymes. Use lots of expressive faces so that baby shares the experience as they listen to your voice and look at your face. Older babies may join in with noises and faces of their own.
Thanks	Thank baby. "Thank you for a lovely listening walk/ lovely song"

QUEST 2: A Toddler QUEST

Magical Mess
of the EYFS

Toddler Activity – Looking at Picture Books You can do this with any picture book but for this example assume you have a picture book about farm animals.	
Question	What can we see in our book?
Understanding	Start off with simple questions to encourage your child to **LOOK/LISTEN** Ask: "Where is the …?" and go through the animals on the page to ensure that your child understands what each animal is **KEYWORD**
Exploring	Begin to explore with further questions such as; Which animal says moo? **WEIGH UP/LOOK/LISTEN** Who do you think lives in that little shed? **INFER** Which animals can fly? **CONNECT** Which animal is the biggest one? **DIVIDE/SIZE** What is that? **QUESTION/RESPOND/KEYWORD** Point to an animal that has black on it **eXEMPLIFY** Which is your favourite animal? Which is the best one? **ZOOM/MAINTAIN** How did that cat get into the tree? **QUESTION/FORMULATE**
Sharing	Now that you have had a chat let your child turn the pages or choose another book. As they chat let them lead the conversation and pop in questions and comments wherever you see the opportunity.
Thanks	Thank your toddler for a lovely time. Mention the things that displayed Thinking Moves skills and the things your toddler seemed to value. For example, "Thank you for sharing your book with me. I really liked it. My favourite animal was the cow. Thank you for showing me your favourite animal, the horse."

QUEST Example: Three to Five-Year-Olds

Toddler Activity - Looking at Picture Books	
You can do this with any picture book but for this example assume you have a picture book about farm animals.	
Question	What can we see in our book?
Understanding	Start off with simple questions to encourage your child to **LOOK/LISTEN** Ask: "Where is the ...?" and go through the animals on the page to ensure that your child understands what each animal is **KEYWORD**
Exploring	Begin to explore with further questions such as; Which animal says moo? **WEIGH UP/LOOK/LISTEN** Who do you think lives in that little shed? **INFER** Which animals can fly? **CONNECT** Which animal is the biggest one? **DIVIDE/SIZE** What is that? **QUESTION/RESPOND/KEYWORD** Point to an animal that has black on it **eXEMPLIFY** Which is your favourite animal? Which is the best one? **ZOOM/MAINTAIN** How did that cat get into the tree? **QUESTION/FORMULATE**
Sharing	Now that you have had a chat let your child turn the pages or choose another book. As they chat let them lead the conversation and pop in questions and comments wherever you see the opportunity.
Thanks	Thank your toddler for a lovely time. Mention the things that displayed Thinking Moves skills and the things your toddler seemed to value. For example, "Thank you for sharing your book with me. I really liked it. My favourite animal was the cow. Thank you for showing me your favourite animal, the horse."

	Would a Worm Make a Good Pet?
	Before starting let the class know that we are having a Philosophy session. Remind the class about the 4Cs that make us good philosophers (Caring – we listen to each other, Creative- everyone has their own ideas and they can be as creative as you want, Critical – we think about what we know and Collaborative – we work as a team to build our ideas)
Question	"I have been wondering... Would a worm make a good pet?" **QUESTION**
Understanding	Learn a little bit about worms either from a book, conversation or You Tube video. **LOOK/LISTEN**
Exploring	Get the children to vote with their feet and go to one side of the room for "Yes a worm would make a good pet" and the other for "No it would not make a good pet" **RESPOND** Some children will remain unsure and you will usually find that these children hover around the middle area unsure of what to do. Address each of these children by name and ask more explicitly "Would you like to have a worm as a pet?" Use their answer to help direct them to the relevant side of the room. **WEIGH UP** Ask a few children from each side to share their reasoning. First remind the children that when you ask the question "why?" you really love it when they use the special word "because" as that lets you know they have really thought about their ideas. Does anyone change their mind as they talk? **JUSTIFY/MAINTAIN/NEGATE**
Sharing	Tell your group that you have now begun to wonder what human jobs a worm would be good or bad at. Would a worm be a good teacher? Would it be a good gardener? Would a worm be a good builder? Would it be a good bus driver? Why/why not? **JUSTIFY/INFER/ZOOM IN/PICTURE/CONNECT/DIVIDE**
Thanks	Thank everyone for their great work today. They are brilliant minibeast explorers! Make a special mention of anyone who has made personal progress today and relate it to a personal achievement or to the 4Cs or the Thinking Moves (depending on your focus for the day) Examples: "Well done ... for listening to your friends today. That was caring." "Well done ...for your great idea about ... That was really creative." "Well done ... for telling me why a worm would make a good gardener. You were great at justifying that."

Chapter 9 – Thinking Moves Synonyms and Related Concepts

I think this would be a good point to give you some handy information from the original Thinking Moves book by Roger Sutcliffe.

Once again, I do urge you to invest in the book as it explains the moves far better than I ever could. I would also like to encourage you to sign up to the DialogueWorks website where you can get a variety of Thinking Moves resources.

The following synonyms and concepts come directly from the Thinking Moves book.

Now that you have seen how Thinking Moves works with children from birth to five-years-old, you will be able to think of so many more ideas and links as you read the following words.

AHEAD: Look forward, expect, hope, target, future, goal, end, means, ambition, risk, precaution, foresight, probable, possible, inevitable, consequence, anticipation, resolution

BACK: recall, rehearse, think again, chew over, beginning, origin, past, history, ancestry, forerunner, memory, recollection, reminiscent, replay, second thoughts, turning point, recollection, reflection,

CONNECT: put together, associate, match, compare, similar, alike, resemblance, identical, relationship. Common, comparison, comparatively, correlation, relevant, analogy. Metaphor, association, assimilation

DIVIDE: tell apart, distinguish, take apart, analyse, different, opposite distinction, exception, contrast whereas, part, element, feature, complex, binary, borderline, differentiation, dissection

EXPLAIN: relate, account for, make clear, define, because, story, narrative, cause, effect, behaviour, motive, law, account, make sense, process, factor, narration, definition

FORMULATE: come up with, express, invent, speculate, idea, draft, concept, brainwave, maybe, guess, intuition, proposal, improvisation, solution, theory, hypothesis, conceptualisation

GROUP: assemble, categorise, label, describe, same, sort, kind, set, class, member, belong, type, species, category, feature, characteristic, organisation, precision

HEADLINE: recap, abridge, condense, outline, heading, point, summary, abstract, digest, gist, in a nutshell, concise, bullet points, synopsise, essence, succinct, concision

INFER: figure out, conclude, interpret, generalise, so, therefore, if...then, follow(s), logic(al), premise, assumption, conclusion, implication, conjecture, (not) necessarily, consistent, deduction, induction

JUSTIFY: say why, excuse, prove, persuade, reasons, excuses, grounds, evidence, position, certainty, proposition, argument, proof, principles, rationale, valid, rationality

KEYWORD: underline, spotlight, emphasise, essentialise, important, main, major, basic, central, essential, core, fundamental, theme. Emphases, memorable, significant, acuteness

LISTEN/LOOK: perceive, observe, apprehend, make sense, senses, aware, alert, perception, sensation, sensitive, observant, environment, information, message, communication, mindful, introspection, attention, comprehension

MAINTAIN: agree, support, hold, assert, belief, claim, true, reality, position, point of view, committed, convinced, value, principle, worldview, axiom, conviction

NEGATE: disagree, object, deny, dispute, wrong, false, negative, opposite, contrary, counter, contradiction, denial, rebuttal, challenge, antithesis, opposition

ORDER: line up, timetable, layout, map, first/next, step/stage, series, plan, method, system, procedure, line, layout, map, coordinates, orderliness

PICTURE: visualise, conjure up, pretend, immerse yourself, scene/scenario, mind's eye, representation, image, vision, model, projection, make-believe, daydream, immersion, in their shoes/place, empathy, imagination

QUESTION: inquire, investigate, puzzle, problematise, where/when/who/why/how/what, open/closed, puzzle, problem, awe, mystery, empirical, research, conceptual, inquiry, leading, rhetorical, inquisitiveness

RESPOND: react, remark, feedback, comment, (dis)like, made me, (I) think, reaction, feeling, emotional, opinion, comment, personal, subjective, view, value, responsiveness

SIZE: count, measure, reckon, figure, all/no(ne), some/most, few/many, number, amount, frequency, fraction, proportion, majority/minority, scale, degree, continuum, sense of proportion

TEST: put in question, make sure, challenge, examine, doubtful, claim, really, sure, questionable, assumption, bias, checklist, mistake(n), testimony, reliable, confirmation, scepticism

USE: try out, put to use, experiment, implement, practical, (in) practice, (in) action, effective, application, function, utility, purpose, implementation, transfer, imitation, pragmatism

VARY: play with, adapt, modify, diversify, different, (an) other, way, perspective, instead, alternative, version, extra, substitution, modification, adaptation, trial and error, adaptability

WEIGH UP: choose, assess, evaluate, deliberate, good/bad, best/worst, right/wrong, (would you) rather, decision, pros/cons, dilemma, balance, impartial, considerations, criteria, verdict, judiciousness

eXEMPLIFY: say (for instance), give an instance, cite, instantiate, example, real-life, event, experience, instance, scenario, case study, typical, sample, exemplar, specimen, citation, groundedness

YIELD: come around to, admit, accommodate, compromise, having heard, on second thought, maybe, negotiation, compromise, deal, adjustment, concession, change of mind, synthesis, self-correction, reconciliation, flexibility

ZOOM IN/OUT: inspect, scrutinise, review, take stock, focus, detail, particular, tiny, aspect, perspective, big picture, overview, general, system, pattern, gestalt, concentration, comprehensiveness

PART 2

THINKING MOVES
IN THE
BIG WIDE WORLD

Chapter 10 – Overcoming Barriers: Special Educational Needs

Many children who cross the paths of Early Years settings will have additional barriers which may make you think that Thinking Moves are not transferable to everyone. In reality, this is not the case. Thinking Moves are so specific but flexible; they can be accessible at any level, and no matter what the barrier to involvement. It is a fully inclusive approach to metacognition and philosophical teaching.

If you work with children who have Severe Learning Difficulties then reducing the number of moves you would like to focus on is a good idea, though you have seen how a majority of them can be done naturally with children at any level of development. For children with less severe Special Educational Needs you can use the Thinking Moves in the same way as you would for any typically developing child, or you could integrate them into their care plans and Individual Education Plans to support specific learning and development that you are working on together. Within my class, I have done Philosophy and used Thinking Moves planning with children at all levels of development and children with a variety of additional needs, from mild to severe. What makes this even more accessible is that each Thinking Move has a British Sign Language action which can be found on the DialogueWorks website. These signs could also be used for Makaton users. The following are some examples of how Thinking Moves could be integrated into Individual Education Plans. You will see that I have split it into areas of need rather than types of diagnosis. This is because so many different disorders, disabilities, and difficulties overlap in what barriers they present so what follows are just a few examples of how children experiencing these difficulties can be supported using Thinking Moves

Sensory Processing Issues

Sensory processing issues are so common and span many different additional needs; however, they are also so varied. No child who has sensory issues is the same as any other, and you will find that sensory processing profiles are very individual and unique to each child. Broadly speaking, though, children will often be over-sensitive or under-sensitive to stimuli. I find it challenging to discuss in such a small section, as this could be a Thinking Moves book all by itself, however, here is a brief look at how Thinking Moves could be included in an Individual Education Plan for sensory issues or used as a parent to support your child.

Much like sensory processing issues, vestibular and proprioceptive awareness (which will usually go hand in hand with other sensory problems) are barriers that can be seen in many different children with many varied additional needs. Vestibular awareness is the ability to know how your body moves, for example, knowing how to go from a standing to a sitting position. Proprioceptive awareness is an awareness of where your body is in space and spatial awareness.

Both of these systems are so much a part of what we are as living beings that the majority of us have well-formed vestibular and proprioceptive systems from being babies and can go our whole lives not even realising they exist. For children with autism or sensory processing issues, there can be issues with their vestibular and processing systems that create a lot of difficulties in navigating everyday life.

If you have never heard of these two words, it is well worth reading about, as vestibular and proprioceptive issues can often go un-recognised, especially in an undiagnosed child or a child not on the autistic spectrum. Here are some examples of how Thinking Moves could be included in an IEP. You will see that these examples are by no means exhaustive, and a real IEP would be broken down into far smaller steps, but hopefully, it will give you some idea as to how Thinking Moves can be used to support a child with sensory issues.

Proprioceptive Issues

Issue or Barrier	Aim or Objective	Thinking Move Support
Proprioceptive Issues X often appears over forceful which can result in hurting others or damaging toys unintentionally. He is generally clumsy and will trip, fall of chairs and walk into objects or other children. He struggles to sit down or stand up without using his hands and can struggle to touch his nose or specific areas with the same ease as his peers. He has poor fine motor skills compared to peers and difficulties with precision movements.	For X to gain a better awareness of his sense of space and improved fine motor skills and to be able to move safely.	X does not seem to sense that he needs support however he does react positively to deep sensory input such as pushing, pulling, hugs, squeezing and lifting heavy objects (CONNECT/USE). Do lost of fine motor activities that require focus (LOOK/LISTEN). Plan AHEAD/FORMULATE so that when X seems to be sensory seeking you can provide safe gross motor and fast activities with acceptable levels of risk . Play games with X where he needs to touch the body part you mention without looking (LISTEN/KEYWORD). Learn the difference between fast/slow and roughly/gently through sensory games (DIVIDE). Provide X with opportunities for climbing and hugs. Set X challenges such as "How quickly do you think you can run to the wall and back? Ready, steady, go!" (SIZE/TEST)

Over and Under Responsive to Stimulii and Vestibular Input

Issue or Barrier	Aim or Objective	Thinking Move Support
Over-responsive to stimuli and vestibular input X does not like noises that are out of her control. She can struggle with bright lights or in sunshine and gets easily over stimulated if there is a lot of noise or activity in the environment. This can lead to over excitement/upset/withdrawal/meltdowns. X does not like certain textures and does not like to get her hands dirty. She has very specific likes regarding what clothes she finds are comfortable. X can also be fearful of movement, for example spinning, swinging and heights. X struggles to listen or concentrate in noisy or busy environments. She will often put her hands over her ears however she also makes noises to herself when playing or when she is meant to be listening to an adult.	For X to be able to identify when she is getting over stimulated and be able to use her own methods and tools in order to manage difficult moments or seek support from an adult.	Support X in being able to **LOOK** and **LISTEN** to identify what is bothering them when they are feeling anxious. When X is in a relaxed state talk to her and see if she can give you examples **(eXEMPLIFY)** of what she dislikes then you can make a plan for supporting X in the future. GROUP them by sound, sight and touch **(KEYWORD)**. Think **BACK**. Can you identify what bothered you the last time you were upset? Think **AHEAD**. What would you like to do if that happens again **(VARY)?** Can X **EXPLAIN** how it makes them feel when they begin to get overwhelmed?
Under- responsive to stimuli and vestibular input X is under sensitive and responsive to outside stimuli. This can sometimes result in him 'thrill seeking' and taking excessive risks without regard for his or other children's safety e.g. climbing onto shelves, running haphazardly, making loud noises, throwing toys, etc. X can often hurt himself but does not realise. X will often engage in sensory play but in an uncontrolled way. This can extend to sensory play which is not planned, for example chewing on sand and mouthing small objects. X either does not react to loud noises or he seeks them out. He likes to make noises such as tapping, humming, whistling. X does not seem distracted in noisy environments.	For X to get the sensory input that he needs but in a safe way.	Encourage X to think of examples **(eXEMPLIFY)** of dangerous things. It is best to do this when X is feeling calm and ready for a chat. Can they **EXPLAIN** why those things might be dangerous. How do they decide if something is dangerous? **(WEIGH UP/TEST)** What does dangerous mean? **(KEYWORD)** What is the difference between safe and dangerous? **(DIVIDE)** What exciting or sensory things does X like to do? What brings him pleasure? **(MAINTAIN)** What safe sensory activities can you plan? **(FORMULATE/AHEAD)**

Language Disorders

Language disorders fit into three main types. With **expressive language disorder,** children have trouble getting their message across when they talk. Their words may come across in the wrong order, or the words they need may not be in their grasp. Children with **receptive language disorder** struggle with their understanding of the language that other people use so can often respond in ways that don't make sense or with preprogrammed phrases or a guess at what the speaker is expecting to hear. Children with **mixed receptive-expressive language** issues can struggle with both using and understanding language. Following are some ways in which Thinking Moves can support children with language disorders.

Social Anxiety

Issue or Barrier	Aim or Objective	Thinking Move Support
Social Anxiety Z won't talk to adults, either directly or in a group situation. He has good levels of using and understanding language as we often overhear him talking to friends during play. His social anxiety can sometimes result in him not seeking adult help when needed. It is also making it increasingly difficult for him to progress in his learning as practitioners are not sure how much he understands or is capable of.	For Z to be able to seek adult support when needed. For Z to begin to talk to a trusted adult - initially on their own terms. For Z to reach their full potential academically.	Provide different options for Z to be able to communicate on his own terms (VARY) such as Makaton, pointing, picture sets, gestures, and facial expressions (eXEMPLIFY/USE/INFER/LOOK). Plan activities in which Z will be able to demonstrate his knowledge and understanding without the need for talking (AHEAD/FORMULATE/VARY/USE) . Ensure small group work is done by carefully selecting the other group members to be ones who contribute to but do not take over conversations in order to leave opportunities open for Z to talk if he wants to (GROUP).

Expressive Language Disorder

Issue or Barrier	Aim or Objective	Thinking Move Support
Expressive language disorder Z has trouble getting her message across when she talks. She often struggles to put words together into sentences that make sense. This results in her struggling to communicate in class and she can become withdrawn or frustrated as a result.	For Z to be able to get her messages across effectively even if she can't think of the correct words to use. For Z to be able to let us know if she is getting frustrated so that we can help.	Practice making short sentences to describe what is going on in a picture or photograph. You can also sit together with a picture book and model this and ask Z to do this on each page by asking "What is happening here?" **(QUESTION/RESPOND/LOOK/ HEADLINE)** Practice using and understanding question words **(QUESTION)** and teach methods such as slowing down and taking three breaths before answering questions so that Z can **FORMULATE** her sentences before she says them. Teach Z alternative ways to get her messages understood such as paraphrasing (VARY) or giving examples **(eXEMPLIFY/CONNECT)**

Receptive Language Disorder

Issue or Barrier	Aim or Objective	Thinking Move Support
Receptive Language Disorder Z struggles to get the meaning of what others are saying. Because of this, she often responds in ways that don't make sense. This is affecting her learning and her ability to keep play going with others. Z also struggles to understand or put names to emotions and to read the facial expressions and non-verbal queues of others.	For Z to be able to understand what is being said to her by having an increased understanding of vocabulary.

For Z to have the confidence to let us know when she doesn't understand something.

For Z to be able to keep play going with her peers. | GROUP words into type then have short vocabulary sessions **(KEYWORD)** to build up schemas of knowledge. Start with areas of interest to Z **(MAINTAIN)** then move on to other areas **(VARY/YIELD)**. Teach Y a few key phrases that she can use when she doesn't understand **(HEADLINE).** These can be phrases to ask for help or to ask for someone to repeat or **EXPLAIN.** Practice asking open questions and encouraging Z to answer or use one of the phrases she has learnt **(QUESTION/RESPOND/USE).** When she does this rephrase until she understands **(VARY)** and congratulate her on using the phrase when she needed it **(WEIGH UP/USE/RESPOND/QUESTION).** Watch Z at play with others and join in. Use this to identify what Z struggles with **(TEST)** so that you can identify her needs and model play **(LOOK/LISTEN)** |

A Need for Routine – Anxiety, and ASD

Many children with Autistic Spectrum Disorder need and have an insistence on sameness and inflexible adherence to routines. This can be right down to the smallest detail of their day, clothing, or placement of a toy. Whereas a neurotypical child will be able to manage flexibility, even if it is sometimes after a tantrum or with a lot of support, this can prove to be a devastating request for a child with autism. Though we cannot, and should not, try to train a child with autism into having the flexibility of routine as a neurotypical child, they do need to be able to eventually manage a certain level of flexibility just to make it through a typical day, and this is where many occupational therapy approaches usually come into play. The following are a selection of commonly used approaches and how these correspond to Thinking Moves

Problems Sequencing Activities or Events.

Issue or Barrier	Aim or Objective	Thinking Move Support
Problems with being able to sequence Y struggles with sequencing in most areas. This can be from the daily sequence (we get up, we brush our teeth, etc) to toileting (often washing his hands before going to the toilet instead of after) and dressing (being unable to dress himself as he is confused about what order to do things.	For Y to be able to sequence common events and activities in his normal day.	Help your child to think BACK to familiar sequences. Make these of an understandable level (SIZE), e.g. a short sequence for younger children such as the order they should put on their socks and shoes or longer ones for older children, building up to being able to ORDER the day ahead for the much older children and teens. The skill of sequencing combines many skills and you can work on each of these by using the chapters in this book to decide on developmentally appropriate activities. The most relevant moves are AHEAD, BACK, FORMULATE, KEYWORD, HEADLINE, ORDER, PICTURE, ZOOM.

A Need to Know What is Going to Happen

Issue or Barrier	Aim or Objective	Thinking Move Support
Need to know what is going to happen Y gets very anxious when there is any uncertainty in what will be happening or when dealing with a new place or situation. This usually results in Y asking the same questions repeatedly, even after being given the answer, and remaining in a state of anxiety until the event happens and unable to get out of their thought pattern to play or talk about anything other than the upcoming event.	For Y to have tools to be able to cope with new, uncertain, or unfamiliar events or places.	After spending some time observing Y **(LOOK/LISTEN),** make a list of anything that you know that makes Y anxious **(FORMULATE/PICTURE).** Plan **AHEAD** for any changes that you can anticipate that will make Y anxious. **GROUP** these into things which can/should be avoided and those which cannot **(CONNECT/DIVIDE).** Also group things by those which you think may be surmountable and those that aren't **(SIZE).** Whenever anything is due to happen that cannot be avoided talk to Y about it in advance. Tell her the **HEADLINE** and also **EXPLAIN** the details **(ZOOM),** including what support you will give and what she should do if she feel nervous **(USE).**

Inflexibility and A Need for a Set Routine

Issue or Barrier	Aim or Objective	Thinking Move Support
Need for a set routine Y has a very set routine both at home and in nursery. If there are any deviations from the routine Y can get very anxious and this can affect the rest of his day or result in meltdowns. Now that Y is getting older there are increasing occasions on which he will need to have flexibility of thought	To be able to create a routine that leaves some room for flexibility and for Y to begin to understand and accept that there will sometimes be occasions where routines change. To give him the emotional tools to be able to deal with this.	Work with Y to talk about what would happen in a normal week and day **(ORDER/EXPLAIN/eXEMPLIFY/ZOOM).** Make a pictorial or photo timetable for the full week **(AHEAD/ORDER/LOOK).** Talk about the things that always happen **(CONNECT)** and the things that might sometimes happen **(DIVIDE/PICTURE). EXPLAIN** why sometimes unexpected things might happen and talk about a plan for what Y can do to stay calm when changes occur **(FORUMULATE/VARY).** Create additional picture cards for any situations you can think of where there may be a change **(PICTURE/USE/VARY)**

Chapter 11 – Overcoming Barriers: English as an Additional Language or Teaching in a Language Other than English

With an approach partly based on learning and understanding new words (26 of them to be exact), it may be a daunting thought to use Thinking Moves with children whose first language isn't English.

If you are working with a mostly English speaking class and the aim for your children is to become English speakers then Thinking Moves works well to be able to teach a new word then give good conceptual understanding through the activity. A far better scaffolding and consolidation than some other approaches would provide.

If you are teaching through a translator or in a classroom in which English is not the primary language used, then this is no barrier either. Thinking Moves is already used across the world in many non-English speaking countries. In these classrooms, each word is translated into the relevant term. It does not matter that the words are no longer literal A-Zs.

In the classroom of Jorge Sánchez-Manjavacas Mellado (http://www.koinefilosofica.org/), the pupils and educators speak Spanish, and so the Thinking Move AHEAD becomes PREVEER ('forsee') and BACK becomes RECORDAR ('remember') but with the same meaning, icon and understanding of those learning it an A-Z in the English Language. So regardless of what language the Thinking Moves are taught in (and what translated words they become) the actual metacognition skills being used remain the same.

Jorge is now working with a Spanish team who are translating the Thinking Moves book into Spanish.

Case Study: Using Thinking Moves in Spanish

By Jorge Sánchez-Manjavacas Mellado

Discovering Thinking Moves and introducing it into my educational space made a big difference. I was what I had been looking for and what I had needed for a long time.

Since I started to teach with a P4C influence, I was always wondering how I can introduce to my students some of the metacognition movements. This book gives us, the teachers, a huge chance to speak about metacognition and how it works in all the dialogues we could have in the class and out, with our families.

As many people know, Spanish schools are becoming more and more bilingual. In all levels, from kindergarten to university level, we are making an enormous effort to grow our educational space into bilingual. For that reason, "TM" could open a lot of opportunities to work on some new vocabulary, questions and mental actions.

During the translation process, we find some problems, like some letters don't fit exactly, but I'm sure we're going to find a solution to do a valuable Spanish translation. As part of a 4-person-team, from País Vasco, Madrid and México city I am currently working on a translation.

In my philosophical dialogues, we always find some problem with naming the actions we usually do when we speak. Especially with teens, because they are often more focused on wanting to say something smart or a delighting idea. For that reason, I find great mental scaffolding in TM and the way it gives this to us: easy to understand and easy to put into practice. To sum up: a book that is worth it.

Maybe all the letters of TM don't fit. But I decided to prove it with some of my students. At the start of a project, I have philosophical dialogues with the teenagers. I found out how well it worked with them. They can anticipate what kind of metacognitive action they are going to do. Even when I asked them to set some questions with every movement, I gave to them. We were talking about the LGTBQ+ community, so all questions were based on this topic. Thinking Moves made our dialogue much better.

Chapter 12 – Overcoming Barriers: Adverse Childhood Events

It is an unfortunate truth that not every child has a rosy, trouble-free childhood. Many children will join Early Years settings, having experienced an Adverse Childhood Event (ACE). This could have led to additional developmental or mental health problems such as Attachment Disorder, Trauma, or Foetal Alcohol Syndrome.

Even children who were very young when their adverse events happened and are now in a happy and settled environment will have questions about their early lives.

For anyone not familiar with the term Adverse Childhood Event here is a definition:

> *"Adverse childhood experiences (ACEs) are traumatic events occurring before age 18. ACEs include all types of abuse and neglect as well as parental mental illness, substance use, divorce, incarceration, and domestic violence. A landmark study in the 1990s found a significant relationship between the number of ACEs a person experienced and a variety of negative outcomes in adulthood, including poor physical and mental health, substance abuse, and risky behaviors.[1] The more ACEs experienced, the greater the risk for these outcomes."*
>
> *https://www.childwelfare.gov*

Though work will often be done with children and their social workers or outside play or talk therapists, helping children with ACEs to learn to use Thinking Moves can provide them with a tool to clarify their thoughts and focus in on what questions they want to ask of their carers or teachers. As they think about their history and current situation and compare it with what they have seen on television or in class as a "normal" family, the Thinking Moves of; Ahead, Back, Connect, Divide, Explain, Question, Respond, Weigh Up, and Zoom can help to focus thoughts and conversations. Thinking Moves can also support talking about emotions.

Amanda Hubball, an early adopter of Thinking Moves, has been doing some amazing work and research into using Thinking Moves to support vulnerable children.

Case Study: Thinking Moves and Vulnerable Children
A Case Study from Alfreton Nursery. By Amanda Hubball

Children in care and those who have been adopted cannot possibly have made it through their life experiences without suffering trauma. Adverse childhood experiences (ACEs) can create barriers in every aspect of a child's life, through into adulthood. As the Designated Teacher for Looked after Children and Adopted Children in school, I have applied Thinking Moves as a tool to enable me to empower children to cope with emotional outbursts, issues around relationships and different aspects of transition. Transitions are commonplace in the life of a child who has suffered breakdowns in attachments. Individual coping strategies mean that communication is not always transparent, and often children are reluctant to expose vulnerability. Equally, when working with such young children, who have already experienced barriers to their emotional development, conscious awareness and thus the ability to articulate vulnerability is often not present.

Work with vulnerable children in school, using Thinking Moves, is an embedded part of practice. As the Mental Health and Well-being Lead in school, I have supported children to break down their emotional responses to situations, through the use of Thinking Moves. There is clearly a subtle interplay between a child's ability to think with compassion and love, feel compassion and love and thus act with compassion and love. The neural pathways for positive and clear thinking need to be strong and resilient if a child who has suffered ACE's has any chance at all of connecting with healthy thinking, prior to reacting under the influence of the amygdala to a perceived threat. The symbiotic relationship between thought and behaviour can be undermined by extreme emotion, thus emphasising more strongly than ever, the need for children to consciously own, understand, control and employ their own thinking, to aid their own well-being. Laying the foundations for children to understand that they have their own voice, their own value and their own power is to give back to a child their capacity for compassionate thought.

*As part of my work in school, I support children to **Listen (and Look)** to themselves and each other. I support **Responding** within themselves and **Explaining** out loud, how they feel and what they think. Children are supported to **Connect** and **Divide** with their peers, fostering empathy and respect for others. **Zooming** in on an individual problem and then zooming out to see other's perspectives, also provides children with a window into their own world and that of their peers. By thinking **Back**, children can reflect on triggers for behaviour and thinking **Ahead** can enable strategy. What could I do differently next time? Supporting children to understand that they think in moves all the time, but they have the power to select those moves whenever they choose, to enable them to better solve a problem, can be a revelation. As children work through these activities they SIZE, JUSTIFY, NEGATE, FORMULATE . . . but for me as the facilitator of these groups, I choose to highlight certain Thinking Moves that I now can be more easily selected by individual children at any given time.*

When our children come to leave the security of our nursery school, ready to move into Primary school, they have once again to cope with loss, transition, uncertainty and 'new'. These events are unavoidable, but I have found that an extra level of support helps both children and adults.

I have put into place a series of online, enquiry based dialogical activities, to support thinking and discourse at home. In school, we have a character called FRED. FRED supports children to understand four key thinking moves: FORMULATE, RESPOND, EXPLAIN and DIVIDE. Through online activities FRED encourages children to think and talk about different aspects of the transition process, aiming to support parents and children to focus their thinking, rather than become overwhelmed with emotion, and open up a communication channel for compassionate and loving enquiry based talk.

An example of one of these activities is as follows. Accompanying this text and image online is a video of me and FRED talking openly about anxiety and how we are feeling.

Week 1

https://www.youtube.com/watch?v=edIlcEl1rAs

https://www.youtube.com/watch?v=jd-dDvsHl60

FRED would like you to sit down with you grown up at home and watch the videos he has sent you. Once you have watched the videos, FRED would like you to look at the questions he has **Formulated** then **Respond** to them. Using the word 'because' FRED would like you to **Explain** to your grown-up what sorts of things worry you. Do you connect with Billy and do lots of worrying, or do you **Divide** and not worry about lots of things at all?

How did Billy feel in the story?

Do you ever feel worried?

What worries you?

Who can you tell if you feel worried?

Can worries be taken away? How? Who by?

When speaking to one Foster mum, she told me, 'Ben hadn't talked about the transition to school at all, so we had assumed he was fine. After speaking to you, we asked him how he was feeling about going to big school. He said he was scared. We were shocked and sad that we hadn't realised. His school visits had gone well, and all talk in the house had been positive – but I guess that was our perception. It's such a relief to have this support, and being able to work clearly through the FRED stages really helps us to stay focused on what Ben needs.'

Thinking Moves is not just about academic success, far from it. Thinking Moves is about creating unity between thinking and feeling. A unity that can support a vulnerable child to become a resilient, empathic and consciously aware adult. Powerless to empowered, voiceless to heard and divided to connected – Thinking Moves is a movement, an evolution of choice, to move from the unconscious to the conscious thinker.

Chapter 13 – Home and Online Schooling With Thinking Moves

In 2020 we all got thrown into a whole new world. It wasn't just in one country; it was a worldwide thing. The COVID19 pandemic hit and all of a sudden teachers had to become online teachers for the first time in their lives, and parents had to home school their children. It wasn't really homeschooling though. Real homeschooling allows for trips out and adventures and parents who can devote their time to homeschooling, not parents who are fitting it in alongside working from home and dealing with all of the other new issues that the pandemic brought along. This was a real test for Philosophy for Children, and Thinking Moves, but it was a hugely successful one. Unlike some more specific subjects which have particular approaches (I have lost track of how many different approaches to mathematics there have been since my childhood days of long division), Philosophy for Children and Thinking Moves proved to be something that anyone could do, with a bit of guidance. It also has the benefit that no textbooks need to be bought or worksheets printed, which made it an inclusive approach to learning which was not reliant on educational background or income. This was a blessing as so many families suddenly had an unexpected reduction in income, and most shops were closed, making it more difficult to source homeschooling supplies.

At my school Philosophy for Children activities were sent home but so too were the amazing weekly 'HomeTalk' sessions which were created by the DialogueWorks team. A lot of teachers also began to deliver their core subjects with a Philosophy for Children slant. Philosophy for Children does not need to be done in a big group and can be done, to an extent, just between a child and their adult within a normal day. The conversational approach to learning creates far more fond memories than sitting down to plough through worksheets with a cursing adult who has to Google things every five minutes because they don't understand what the question their child is being asked even means.

Thinking Moves also created a vehicle for being able to discuss emotional and new issues (for most children) relating to our societal responsibilities, our personal responsibilities, not being able to see loved ones, loss, and grief. It also gave teachers some tools to prepare to support children on their return to school. In the midst of all of this, we also saw Black Lives Matters protests across the western world, and Philosophy for Children and Thinking Moves gave us the tools to be able to discuss these with our children.

If you are a homeschooler or planning for children at school and at home then you should visit the HomeTalk and the Early Years resources to help children deal with uncertain times on the DialogueWorks website (https://dialogueworks.co.uk/young-children/). If you work through these, then you will find that by the end of them you can consider yourself a bit of a Thinking Moves expert.

Amanda Hubball found great success with her lockdown online schooling, as you will see in our next case study.

Online Learning using Thinking Moves.

A Case Study from Alfreton Nursery School By Amanda Hubball

The COVID 19 pandemic has certainly changed the way education looks, feels and more importantly, how it is accessed. At the same point as our primary mode of educational delivery moved to being online, our primary vehicle for teaching was handed over to parents. Accessibility became essential, and both parents and children as both needed to be able to enjoy and understand education in a very new way.

Thinking Moves became a critical tool which was effectively employed to support in the delivery of our early years curriculum, particularly maths. The specific thinking moves which were used as a thinking groove in maths had already been established in school, prior the pandemic. However, as the implementation of this new approach was still in its infancy, the move to 'online learning' provided an opportunity to get the new 'metacognitive maths' approach, creatively implemented and embraced by all stakeholders.

Maths QUESTSs became a daily part of our online learning offer, and parents and children embraced the approach. A short video clip accompanied every lesson, setting the scene and articulating the quest for the day. The maths teacher would pose a **Question** for the day, linked to certain mathematical skills and understandings that children needed to learn. From the starting point of a question, there was then a breakdown of thinking moves that children would need to work through, in order to arrive at the answer. Children were asked to **Use** their thinking and counting skills along with resources found at home. They were then encouraged to **Explain** their work and their thinking to the grown-up at home, enabling a supportive and open dialogue between parent and child. **Sizing** was a critical element to the thinking groove, as children were asked to consider the size and accuracy of their work. Possibly the most essential part of the QUEST process came in the form of the final element, **Test**. As children began to realise the importance of testing their findings to establish validity, parents embraced the concept too.

During weekly well-being phone calls to parents, there was very positive feedback about the Maths QUESTs and how effective these little thinking grooves had proven to be for children and parents alike. Adults reported finding the simplicity and clarity of the process accessible and easy to use to teach their children maths. Children loved working through a short and clearly focused lesson, with an obvious beginning, exciting middle and very clear end. One parent told me:

'The first thing Sam very excitedly said to me when he woke up this morning was, 'Is there another maths quest today mummy?''

More feedback from the parent of a little girl was: 'To our, amazement Abbey came into the kitchen today and announced that she was off to size her toys to make sure she'd got them in the right order'.

Children were beginning to use the language of Thinking Grooves, and Thinking Moves naturally in their home talk. One mum said, 'Daisy is mesmerized by the quests. She just watches them over and over again before disappearing off and returning ten minutes later with the answer.'

A dad told me that his son now understood much more clearly the process of explaining. He said it had never occurred to him that 'explaining something' was not a concept his son had understood with clarity. But through applying the concept to a Thinking Groove, his son could suddenly see the explicit nature, meaning and purpose of this previously taken for granted, act.

As we began to open our school up slowly to more children, some of them came in with the Thinking Moves language. One little girl said as soon as she saw me at the gate, 'I can do maths quests, I can. I love doing them cos they help me learn numbers and cos it means mummy stays with me and we do it together.' Is there a more powerful acknowledgement of the value of providing the tools of education in a respectful and transparent way, enabling parents to participate in the process of learning with their children? Thinking Moves had proven to be a huge motivator for learning in our school, during a period of time when uncertainty, pressure and fear surrounded the concept of home education for millions the countrywide.

The Hubball Thinking Moves QUEST Model

Question	Pose a **QUESTION** for the day, linked to certain mathematical skills and understandings that children need to learn. Give a breakdown of thinking moves that children will need to work through, in order to arrive at the answer.
Use	Ask children to **USE** their thinking and counting skills along with resources found at home.
Explain	Encourage children to **EXPLAIN** their work and their thinking to their teacher or parent, enabling a supportive and open dialogue
Size	**SIZING** is a critical element to the thinking groove, as children are asked to consider the size and accuracy of their work.
Test	Children begin to realise the importance of **TESTING** their findings to establish validity

Chapter 14 – Growing Up: Essential Philosophical Thinking for Older Children and Teens

So what is the point in doing this approach with children from such a young age? Is it worth the bother? It is essential that we teach our children to be more analytical, creative, and independent thinkers, now more than ever and we only need to look at the world that our older children and teens are growing up in to see why.

Between the news, our fast-moving society, and social media, children are getting involved in the world from a much younger age. Even equipped with all of the teachings that primary school and secondary schools have to throw at them, it remains a concern. With little in most curriculums, which fosters critical thinking, analytical skills, imagining different scenarios, and making their own decisions, children are often sent off into the world without adequate emotional or mental tools to make the adult decisions expected of them.

"Don't trust men in white vans and stay away from strangers" we say. "Don't go on this app or that one", "If you are a girl dress conservatively or beware. If you are a boy, you are born with no impulse control, so this is what you need to remember while you fight those natural urges". But, of course, none of that is accurate or vaguely helpful. Bad guys don't always come in white vans; sometimes, they are not even male. Strangers aren't always bad, and the people who might hurt you are not always strangers. This or that app might be dangerous, but new ones pop up every day, and bad people find new ways to exploit innocence on the internet (and children and teens find new ways to hide things from their parents). Girls who dress a certain way are not "asking for it", and boys are not all born with the urge to hurt people and lack of impulse control. What dangerous and offensive nonsense those archaic stereotypes are!

These over generalisations, that parents and educators sometimes give to try to protect our children are bordering on useless when taught in isolation. We should be teaching children what to look out for to stay safe from danger, but even we do not know many of the signs until they have been reported on the news and they don't always get reported in the news until a few terrible incidents have happened. In that case, teaching facts and assumptions is not enough. To help children navigate the world in safety and make the choices that lead them to have a happy and fulfilled life we need to teach them how to make those choices when there are no adults around to ask (or when they wouldn't ask anyway even if one was sitting right next to them). We need to teach them how to think critically and creatively and consider all options and possibilities when making their choices.

Our teens and children are also growing up in a world with juxtaposing parts of society. On the one hand, we are getting better as a society at being more accepting, understanding and tolerant of each other; yet, on the other hand, there are increasing pockets of society with destructive beliefs about gender, sexual orientation, race, religion and so many other elements of our world. Unfortunately, it is often the least savoury voices that shout the loudest and so systemic inequalities and discrimination in every sense of the word continue to thrive. It is unfortunate that these voices can often come from people in positions of power. This makes it, even more, essential that we equip our teens with the necessary thinking skills to pull apart the flaws in arguments and opinions to find their own way to better truths and so build a more beautiful world.

Gone are the days when we lived in naïve optimism until puberty hit and the only news we got was pretty accurately reported on the BBC. Children are now getting social media accounts from a young age (despite the recommended ages of 13). We have even built internet safety and other adult concerns like terrorism into our primary curriculum. Gone are those days where children can just listen to their parents and teachers and get that good grounding of fact-based knowledge before they hit their teens and here are the days that they need to start digesting, processing, and forming their own ideas based on a barrage of conflicting opinions.

Life moves fast! For a few years the, very famous You Tuber, Logan Paul, was seen as a 'safe' influence. His brother was even a Disney channel regular until the channel "mutually agreed" to separate themselves from him. Skip a few years forwards, and Logan Paul's videos take a turn as they begin to objectify women and, of course, his now infamous and callous visit to the Japanese "suicide forest". But at what point do the parents of his pre-teen fans decide that he is no longer appropriate? Before his inappropriate turn? Well, that isn't possible, so by the time parents stop their child from watching You Tubers like this, their child has already seen many videos that challenge their way of seeing the world. Our flawed information doesn't just come from former teen stars. Even people in the most elevated positions of politics and power have proved themselves during the COVID19 crisis as being, at best liars and, at worst truly idiotic (a cup of bleach to cure COVID anyone?). If the adults around them haven't given them the skills to take in information and opinions and make considered judgments, then children are left being influenced by no-longer safe idols.

Another part of the world children are experiencing is the increasing threat of terrorism. When I was young, there were still acts of terrorism around the world, but it was not yet at the scale that we see now and not such a part of a child's world. It happened. It was in the newspaper, on the radio, and on one of the three or four news programmes that were on grown-up TV at some point during the day. It did not intrude, too much, into most children's lives or consciousness. It was a grown-up concern.

Children nowadays are experiencing terrorism and gaining an awareness of it from a much younger age. After the bombing of the Arianna Grande concert in Manchester in 2017, four of the children in my class(three-year-olds) mentioned it during registration. This was the next morning. Less than twelve hours after it had happened. They mentioned it as soon as I reached their names in the register and burst out with the tiny bits of information that had already seeped into their little brains. All of a sudden, I was faced with three children who knew about the bombing and twenty-three children who were now wondering what was being talked about and were eager to hear more. There was an assembly about it too. My class didn't go, they were far too young for a 20-minute assembly even if it wasn't on such a sad and scary issue, but their siblings did. Some parents chose to tell their children about the bombing, and some didn't, but the children were a part of the world. A world where information comes from all avenues, and where even Disney Channel icons can end up amid a terrorist situation. How can you even hope to explain these things to a three-year-old?

Not only are the children that we teach now exposed to more videos and news about terrorism we even actively have PREVENT training for teachers to spot the early signs of extremism and radicalisation that we may see in children. It isn't just the ISIS-style extremism either. In a turbulent society, there is also radicalisation coming from the white supremacist front. How can we expect children, who are only just becoming aware of death (never mind processing the reality of it) and whose most significant conflict is usually about not wanting to brush their teeth before bed, to be able to understand and process the existence of terrorism?

A Thinking Moves approach to teaching does not give all of the answers but what it does do is help to create a mindset from a young age which provides children with the tools to take in information which is often conflicting (and sometimes fake) and opinions and create their own. That is the key. The view and ideas that we all have are precisely that. Our own. So it is up to us to give our children the tools to be able to form their own opinions, taking account of everything they have heard and read, without being overwhelmed or brainwashed by the most vocal opinions. If we create little philosophers then hopefully they can create a positive future for us all.

Children are a bundle of emotions that they often can't explain. Do we think we have it bad as adults? Well, children have it ten times worse. They can go through a myriad of emotions all in the same day and, usually, have no control over either the emotions (hello terrible twos and teenage hormones) or the events that led to them (missed the bus, lost a toy, boring lesson, fell out with a friend, lost their PE kit and so on). For toddlers and young children, the bad moods are usually fleeting and quickly replaced with a good one, but for pre-teens and teens they can often feel like a bottle of coke that has been shaken so many times over the day (forgot a book *shake*, told off for talking in class *shake*, the kid next to me in class kept kicking my chair *shake*) that your seemingly unoffensive comment of 'homework time' is just that final shake that makes their coke bottle of emotions explode and flow over with no hope of pushing them back into the emotional bottle. We can't help with all of these little shakes the way we did when they were younger. The best we can do is teach them coping skills.

I know we were all young once, we have all gone through these stages of growing up, and we survived, but I think the youth of today get a hard deal. Yes, they have the miracle of technology that we never had, and most likely, they have more money and are more spoilt than we were at their age. There are more restaurants, takeaways, television options, and entertainment venues for them than there were for us. Life is sweet. Except it isn't. I am so happy that I grew up without the social pressures that the internet has brought. I am not here to criticise the internet by any means – there are so many amazing things that it offers both on superficial and deep levels – but it makes growing up hard.

The pressures on children and teens to look a certain way and act a certain way are immense. So many children and teens now measure their physical attractiveness and worth in comparison to the latest Instagram stars and trends and measure their popularity in 'likes'.

Teens and pre-teens are suffering from anxiety, depression, body issues, cyberbullying, and a fear of missing out as a result of social media. There is also the ever-present risk of grooming and radicalisation. Before the internet, these were things which were the rare exception for children and not so much a norm that schools had to run regular refresher training for teachers to be able to be on the lookout for. Issues that were previously the territory mainly of older teens and adults are now being experienced by much younger people who have much less life experience and less developed coping skills.

Children and teens are being shown people with seemingly perfect lives, immaculate bodies, and expensive things and, due to the sheer number of social media account holders doing this, being given the impression that this is normal. That it is what they should be aspiring to and if they don't measure up, then they are a failure. They are being put into a 'grass is always greener, and I will never be that good' mindset which can leave them feeling like they can't achieve happiness unless they have that money, that body, and that number of followers.

As children enter their teens with social media all around them but not the foresight that adults hopefully have (but let's face it we usually don't), they are opening themselves up to tiny actions that can have lifelong effects. How many of today's teens will end up struggling to get the job they want or the relationship they want because of all of the digital skeletons in their past that are no longer in the closet? The photos of them doing something stupid at age twelve that went viral or the rumour that was started about them on Facebook that went around the whole school. I am so thankful that my teen years were not captured on social media. In giving children and teens social media, with 24-hour access for those with mobile phones, we have taken our children and put them in the deep dark woods without a map, compass, or torch to help.

My greatest wish for my children and the children I teach is that when they see trends and trendsetters on social media they will have the clear-mindedness, independence, and confidence to be able to filter real from unreal and important from superficial mentally. I hope that if they ever find themselves in a potentially dangerous situation (grooming, cyberbullying, radicalisation, peer-pressure, and all of the other worries that parents of teens have) that they have the critical thinking skills to realise that danger and do the right thing and the creative skills to get out of those situations. We can't be there all the time. We have so little control that it is truly terrifying. Children can become trolls, encouraged, and swept along by more forceful friends and the anonymity of the internet. Children can be sitting in the same room as you or in their bedroom being cyberbullied without you even knowing it.

In addition to all of these pressures, we also now have 'fake news'. I know many adults who can't even discriminate between fake and real news. Just have a peep on your Facebook feed now if you have them. How many people are sharing or commenting on four-year-old stories that were proved to be myths many years ago as if they were today's news? How many people are asking you to share or like a post and if you don't then you definitely have proved that you support cancer, child slavery, and kicking kittens (and don't forget the pressuring and slightly peevish claim on each one that 'I bet 92.7% of people won't share this post'). Then there are the 'no-one wished this little boy happy birthday because he is disabled' posts prompting you to wish him a happy birthday and always fake.

Then it gets even sneakier because anyone can edit Wikipedia or write a blog or opinion piece now and it can be on the internet in seconds. So children who are just starting to use the internet and who are used to everything that is the written word and being presented by an adult being trusted facts, now have the job that some adults can't manage – the task of filtering what is real from what isn't. Even politicians are caught out daily in lies or ill-informed fake news. What hope do they have of surviving to adulthood without becoming misinformed fools? Our only hope is to teach them to be able to think through things logically and begin to make these distinctions themselves.

A Philosophy for Children approach to parenting can help children to gain the skills they need to survive the online world unscathed, or relatively so. Of course, I am not a teenager myself, so what do I know? So I asked a teenager who has been using Philosophy for Children from an early age whether all of this seemed true and this is what she had to say.

Quote from Ella Parker, aged 13:

> "I found this chapter quite relatable. It feels like I've experienced all of the things it talks about, and that just shows proof of how dangerous things like social media can be."

It seems only fitting that our final case study is from Gina Parker Mullarkey, Ella's mum, Thinking Moves trainer, and the person who trained me in my first steps into P4C and trains all of the Early Years teachers in my school as they take their first steps into P4C too.

Case Study: Growing up with a Philosophy for Children Trainer

By Gina Parker Mullarkey and Ella Parker

I first came across Philosophy for Children (P4C) when I was studying for my PGCE over 20 years ago, thanks to the wonderful Chris Rowley. My career moved from a classroom teacher very quickly to a P4C trainer, whilst still linking back to my roots as an outdoor educator. I had the privilege of working at Cumbria Development Education Centre for over 15 years, where through many projects, I was able to explore the value of P4C linked to Global Education. My children, Zac now seven years and my daughter Ella, now 13 years were if I am honest my Guinea pigs (a pet they would still like, but I haven't succumbed to) and it seems they know that!

The impact of P4C upon my own children became more apparent with my second child, largely due to my daughter pointing this out to me! We talk about the value of family mealtimes a lot, and it became very evident that these were naturally a time for great philosophical dialogue. I should hasten to point out that these conversations weren't led by me, as a parent my priorities at breakfast were very different 'eat-up', 'where's your school bag?' and 'hurry we are going to be late for school/work', but it seems through my questioning of their statements, modelling of questions and probing of their ideas they were keen to share and lead philosophical dialogues themselves. I am pleased that my second child has given me the opportunity to observe this impact more fully. I recorded some fantastic examples over mealtimes with him and found that my daughter had become the facilitator to his inner dialogues as I had been for her.

We talk about a stimulus for a P4C enquiry, broadly defined as 'something to get us thinking' and it was amazing even at the age of 4, how he found his own stimuli naturally without interference from me. The breakfast bowl example is one of my favourites, which led to a fantastic enquiry over breakfast exploring the concept of happiness, and we still made it to school and work on time! Other questions included; Why do people die? Why do we need pounds in the world? How do we know what a baddy is? and Why are there germs in the world? Such big questions at the age of 3-4 years.

Is that a happy smile?

My daughter it seems enjoys philosophy, and when I mentioned that I was reflecting on the impact of P4C on my own children, as an aspiring writer, she wrote me a quick paragraph.

"As a teen, I think that Philosophy for Children influences me more than I realise. I now enjoy challenging my thinking (and not just because it can annoy my parents). I think it also helps me to be a bit more creative with the way I think about the world." - Ella Parker

This truly made me smile and yes, she 'challenges' us all the time as a teenager!

As a family, we love being in the outdoors, which has provided numerous opportunities for P4C. One of my daughter's regular activities is to come up with 'Would you rathers?' when we are out walking, many inspired by the environment around us, examples have included 'Would you rather be a worm or a slug? Or 'Would you rather be the funniest or wisest person?' We have even collected items as a family and ordered them from most to least!

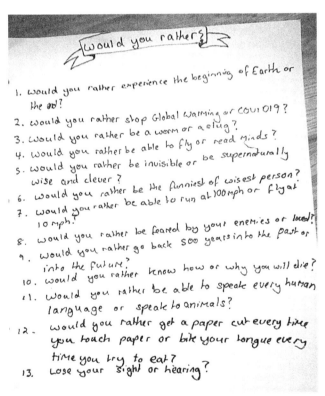

Would you rather?

1. Would you rather experience the beginning of Earth or the end?
2. Would you rather stop Global Warming or COVID19?
3. Would you rather be a worm or a slug?
4. Would you rather be able to fly or read minds?
5. Would you rather be invisible or be supernaturally wise and clever?
6. Would you rather be the funniest of wisest person?
7. Would you rather be able to run at 100mph or fly at 10mph?
8. Would you rather be feared by your enemies or loved?
9. Would you rather go back 500 years into the past or into the future?
10. Would you rather know how or why you will die?
11. Would you rather be able to speak every human language or speak to animals?
12. Would you rather get a paper cut every time you touch paper or bite your tongue every time you try to eat?
13. Lose your sight or hearing?

Some examples of 'Would you Rather's' by Ella Parker

I would, of course, say with no bias that P4C has had an extremely positive effect on my children who I consider to be extremely articulate, reflective, considerate and creative, but of course, there is research out there which highlights the benefits of P4C with a much larger research base. If I was to recommend one tool for parents linked to P4C, I would say ask good questions to support your children in considering and furthering their thinking.

I recently wrote an article examining good questioning linked to the outdoors *Reflective Tea Drinking – Forest School, Philosophy for Children and the Questionable Question of Questions'* so please do take a peek at this. (1)'

Perhaps you would like to involve your family in P4C? I will leave you with a question developed by my daughter with some of her initial thinking to get you started!

Are there more colours than what humans can see?

So, we see with the colours red, orange, yellow, green, blue, purple and pink with different shades of each colour, right? Then there's black and white (shades) and other colours you can make with the main colours such as turquoise and magenta. Well, what if there were more colours? If you think about it, there's nothing saying that couldn't be true! Other animals can see different colours to us, like dogs seeing in blue, yellow and grey, so what's there to say we are missing out on some colours to?

If we can't see these possible colours, could there be other animals that do? If not, could they actually be counted as colours if nobody can see them?

 o *Question and thinking by Ella Parker*

(1) 'Reflective Tea Drinking – Forest School, Philosophy for Children and the Questionable Question of Questions' was published in the Institute for Outdoor Learning Horizons journal in the summer of 2020. This article can be accessed by visiting www.littlechatters.co.uk/resources

Appendix 1: Progression of Thinking Moves From Birth to Five

Thinking Move	Babies	Toddlers	Three to Five Year Olds
AHEAD	Talk about your daily routine	Anticipation games such as blowing bubbles or tickling games. Introduce future tense words	Introduce more future words and the concept of time in the future (tomorrow, next week, next year). Encourage your child to plan ahead for small tasks and longer term activities or events.
BACK	Talk about what happened in the immediate past (last few seconds or minutes)	Talk about what happened in the further past. Introduce past tense words and phrases such as "last time" and "remember"	Refer to past experiences in relation to present ones. Ask questions about stories you have read or things you have previously said.
CONNECT	Basic labelling of common things e.g. different pictures of 'cats'	Tidying toys into same and different. Learning things that connect (all cars) and divide (basket of cars and basket of books)	Play Odd One Out games. Talk about similarities and differences between them and their friend or their families and other families.
DIVIDE	Look at opposites and demonstrate them e.g. high/low, loud/quiet		
EXPLAIN	Talk about things as they happen	Encourage toddlers to verbalise	Play positional language games where a child has to explain to you where to find something. Encourage children to explain things fully to you in everyday life and don't make assumptions or paraphrase for them unless you need to.
FORMULATE	Provide challenges during tummy time or with items just out of reach	Create problem solving opportunities and introduce problem solving games	Create more advanced problem solving games and opportunities which include barriers and a need for more creative thinking.
GROUP	Group three toys at a time by type, size or colour	Similar to connect/divide – group toys or objects by type, colour, size or whether you like them or not	Group by more detailed or complex properties. Group by abstract concepts. Introduce Venn grouping

Thinking Move	Babies	Toddlers	Three to Five Year Olds
HEADLINE	Give one sentence explanations	Simplify sentences to their essential parts. Give overview of each page of a picture book and eliminate all unnecessary words	Introduce the phrase "Give me the headline" and "What is the headline?" Reduce each page of a book that you are reading to a short headline.
INFER	Talk about cause and effect – this happened so that must be true	Games with clues and hints e.g. "What animal lives here? It eats grass and says mooo"	Learn to read clues in pictures and facial expressions. Read clues from what people say and from the things they see.
JUSTIFY	Talk about justifications in what you do – I am doing this because...	Regularly use the words "why" and "because"	Ask your child "Why?" and "Why do you think...?" Initiate conversations about the world and play ignorant "I was just wondering why...?"
KEYWORD	Label things to teach new words.	Put two key words together Introduce keyword games	Ask children to recall all of the keywords they have learnt about a topic. When a child is struggling to explain something work together to pull out the keywords.
LOOK/LISTEN	Introduce the words "look" and "listen"	Learn the difference between looking and listening on a listening walk	Build the ability to be 'active listeners'. Build the ability to look at and listen to things not based on their personal interests. Look and listen to adults and peers and the natural world. Use listening skills in the introduction of phonics.
MAINTAIN	Teach the word "yes"	Play yes and no games	Support children in being brave enough to maintain their own opinions and beliefs in the face of opposition.
NEGATE	Teach the word "no"		Play the "But What If...?" game to teach your child how to deal with negation. Practice negating with justifications

Thinking Move	Babies	Toddlers	Three to Five Year Olds
ORDER	Use ordinal language in everyday tasks (1st, 2nd, next, then, finally, last, etc)	Model ordering things by size. Continue to use ordinal language	Order by more detailed properties of abstract concepts. Introduce concept lines. Sequence events, activities and stories.
PICTURE	Talk about things that can't be seen e.g. talk all about cats – what they look like and what they do	Talk about what people might be doing (grandma, postman, etc) Ask toddler to describe things using questions (What colour is a pig? How many legs does it have?)	Picture the details of future events. Teach children how to picture how another child may think or feel. Picture alternative endings or details. Get children to picture something and describe it.
QUESTION	Ask questions throughout the day to teach baby how our voice inflects when we ask a question e.g. "Should we get some milk? Yes let's get some milk"	Model 'why' and 'because' in everyday speech. Turn one or two word comments that the toddler makes into questions (Child: 'blankie' Adult: 'Where is your blankie?')	Teach the difference between questions and information. Teach question words who, what, where, when, why, and how. Play the 'What is it?' game.
RESPOND	When baby coos or makes a noise copy the noise back. Do the same with copying faces. Do noises and faces yourself to see if baby copies	Encourage the toddler to copy the noises you make. Sing nursery rhymes but leave out the last word of each line for your toddler to fill in. Begin to ask questions and wait for an answer.	Ask lots of questions. Value answers. Aim to have dialogues with children that last for at least ten back and forth interactions.
SIZE	Use the language of size in everyday life	Introduce a broader range of size words	Work on counting and subitizing (estimating accurately). Introduce more language of size. Learn to estimate time.

Thinking Move	Babies	Toddlers	Three to Five Year Olds
TEST	Use the words test and use in everyday life as you test things and say what use they have or how you will test things	Introduce open-ended problem-solving games and resources	Get children to volunteer ideas about how to test real life suggestions and what tests could be done to find out the truth of conceptual questions.
USE		Role play with themed activity baskets and play with open ended items giving one item several uses (e.g. a cup can be a cup, tub, shoe, hat, phone, etc)	Introduce the phrase "Let's use what we know" and use this in a variety of ways. Look at various uses of objects – who would use a …?
VARY	Introduce different foods, ways of using your voice and ways of using toys.	Vary foods, routines, trips, and uses for toys. When your toddler tries at something but fails support them in varying their approach.	Change well known stories. Play 'But what if…? Encourage varying approaches when something doesn't work.
WEIGH UP	Talk as you weigh up the choices yourself. "Which top should I put on you today? Let's have this one because it is nice and warm"	Give your toddler choices throughout the day. Talk about good and bad decisions.	Encourage children to make considered choices about what to do in different hypothetical situations and throughout the day.
eXEMPLIFY	Look at books with examples of one specific item in them e.g. a picture book all about cars or colours	Encourage your toddler to vocalise what they want or use pointing or gestures. Begin to talk about examples of a wider range of items e.g. instead of examples of cars talk about vehicles	Look at 'setting an example' and exemplary behaviour or values. Encourage children to give or imagine examples of situations and emotions.

Thinking Move	Babies	Toddlers	Three to Five Year Olds
YIELD	Interrupt baby when they are making noises to make your own noises/say something – teaching turn taking. Persist with new experiences even if baby rejects them the first time.	Introduce rules and boundaries for your house or setting. Encourage sharing. Offer new items that you know would not be the toddler's first preference.	Teach negotiation without conflict. Get children to consider other people's opinions. Teach children that other people do not have to have the same opinion as them.
ZOOM	Focussing on faces and bold or bright prints and colours – particularly high contrast colours like black and white.	Practice zooming in by looking at and talking about each page of a picture book for longer than you usually would.	Zoom in to one small element or person when looking at pictures or picture books. Zoom in to consider what one person may be feeling or thinking. Zoom in to learn all about one thing. Zoom out to see the bigger picture or consider other points of view. Use zooming in and out to direct focused learning.

Appendix 2: A Chat With My Four Year Old at Bedtime

Here is an example of how you can use Thinking Moves to structure a chat.

AHEAD: What would you like to do tomorrow?

BACK: Can you remember anything that we did today?

CONNECT: What can we do tomorrow that is the same as something that we did today?

DIVIDE: What can we do that is different?

EXPLAIN: Can you tell me more about that?

FORMULATE: Let's plan out the day

GROUP: Let's group things into the things we want to do for fun and the things we have to do

HEADLINE: What did we do at the park today?

INFER: What time of day do you think it is now?

JUSTIFY: Why do you think it is nighttime?

KEYWORD + LISTEN/LOOK: Let's listen very carefully. What can you hear? Can you see anything?

MAINTAIN: Why is bedtime nice?

NEGATE: I know you don't want to go to sleep, but you have to!

ORDER: Let's talk about what we will do in the morning before we play/go to school

PICTURE: What sort of weather do you think we will have tomorrow?

QUESTION: Do you have any questions?

RESPOND: I have a question for you…

SIZE: How quickly do you think you will be able to get dressed in the morning? How many slices of toast will you eat?

TEST: How can we test to see if you are right?

USE: What can we use to time how quickly you get dressed?

VARY: What different things could we put in your packed lunch?

WEIGH UP: You can't have all of those things! Which are your favourite things for your packed lunch?

eXEMPLIFY: Can you tell me what animals come out at night?

YIELD: It is time to go to sleep now.

ZOOM OUT/IN: We are in a big universe with lots of planets and stars and the moon. We are on the planet earth. We are in a continent called... We are in a country called... Our town is called... We live on ... Street. We are in our cosy house. We are in your bedroom. We are in a comfortable bed, wrapped up snug and warm. We have our head on our pillows. We are closing our eyes and going to sleep to have a lovely dream. Night, Night.

Appendix 3: Thinking Moves Training

While Thinking Moves A – Z is remarkably easy to access, it is worth teachers and other educators investing in some training in the use of the framework. This will ensure that you know how to establish it in the right way, and that you understand how to get the most out of it for your students. Once you've done the training, you'll be ready to use it in class straightaway – and you'll also have a vision of how to develop it over the longer term.

DialogueWorks offers an introductory Thinking Moves A- Z training course that will:

- o Familiarise you with Thinking Moves A – Z and show you different ways to introduce it to your students so that they can quickly memorise and own it;
- o Show you how to enrich inquiry-based learning programmes, such as Philosophy for Children, by incorporating Thinking Moves;
- o Show you how to build Thinking Moves into the main curriculum, or into specialist thinking skills, study skills and life skills courses;
- o Give you practical guidance on how to embed Thinking Moves A – Z in your school's overall approach to teaching and learning.

The format of the training is flexible: it can be a single full day, two-half days or three twilight sessions – online or in-person. DialogueWorks offers it on a whole-school basis for teams of up to 25 teachers, or for individual teachers on open courses. They can provide bespoke courses for applications outside mainstream school, such as parent groups, vocational or professional training and life-skills organisations. All the trainers are accredited in Thinking Moves A – Z - and they can offer their training worldwide.

DialogueWorks also offer a course called 'Whole School Values, Whole Person Virtues' which is a six hour course run over three two hour sessions.

For details of training courses and resources, please refer to www.dialogueworks.co.uk: or you can just search for "Thinking Moves A – Z training".

Appendix 4: Organisations Paving the Way to The Future of Philosophy for Children

DialogueWorks and Roger Sutcliffe's Thinking Moves

Founded by Bob House, Roger Sutcliffe, and Nick Chandley, DialogueWorks provides training, support, and resources in teaching that brings more thinking into learning. DialogueWorks has two main programmes. P4C Plus is an approach that embeds P4C across all teaching and learning to create a philosophical teaching and learning approach. In addition to working with the six strands of philosophical teaching, P4C Plus also includes the second programme – Thinking Moves.

On the DialogueWorks website, you can find access to resources and training, both online and in person. Roger Sutcliffe (creator of Thinking Moves) is one of the world's leading authorities on P4C and philosophical education. He was a founder and President of SAPERE, the UK charity promoting P4C, and President of ICPIC, the International Council for Philosophical Inquiry with Children. He graduated in Philosophy and Modern Languages at Oxford and has taught at primary and secondary levels. He trained in P4C under Professor Lipman.

Nick Chandley is a qualified teacher and has led numerous P4C courses, at Foundation and Advanced levels and from Early Years to FE colleges. Well-known for 'squeezing the juice', he edited a P4C training handbook and co-edited *P4C through the Secondary Curriculum* (Continuum, 2012). Nick has trained several P4C Gold Award schools and has presented at conferences on topics as diverse as raising standards in English through P4C and P4C with parents. Nick helped develop and write the hugely successful *What's the Big Idea?* TV series, now sold to over 100 countries worldwide, and was an education consultant to the major documentary series *The World According to Kids* (BBC2) and to *Feeling Better* (CBeebies). This show helps young children manage their emotions.

Bob House studied Economics and has an MBA from INSEAD, France. He worked as a strategy consultant before moving into the education sector. Bob was CEO of SAPERE from 2012 – 16. He set up the Education Endowment Foundation's trial of the effectiveness of P4C and the Nuffield Foundation's research into the non-cognitive benefits of P4C.

Bob has advised DialogueWorks' clients, such as P4C China and Baseera Al-afkar Corporation, on how to establish and grow their P4C training organisations from a commercial and operational perspective.

https://dialogueworks.co.uk/

Baseera

Baseera is an education consultancy based in Jeddah, Saudi Arabia which uses internationally-accredited programs to introduce philosophical thinking and Socratic dialogue as a basis for developing learning tools, pedagogy, and the educational environment

.The term "Baseera" draws its root from the depth of Islamic philosophical tradition. "basar: vision", "Baseera: foresight" and "tabasor: considering carefully" all refer to the concept of the wise person or the philosopher.

Baseera offers educational services specialized in P4C to schools and universities as well as evening services for enrichment programs and after-school activities. In Saudi Arabia and the Arab world, they provide P4C training in collaboration with DialogueWorks. They have received international accreditation from both SAPERE and The Philosophy Foundation.

Baseera started in 2011 as a pioneer experimental program in Saudi Arabia and the Arab world, to provide philosophical thinking for children, young people, and adults as an enriching and extra-curricular activity before becoming an educational and pedagogical consultancy in 2018. Baseera aims to encourage self-confidence in the Baseera community as well as providing guidance and development to help teachers, students, and everyone it works with reach their fullest potential.

You can find out more about the work of Baseera and their team at http://baseera.com.sa

International Council of Philosophical Inquiry with Children (ICPIC)

The ICPIC was established in 1985 to oversee biennial conferences and expand the reach of P4wC (Philosophy for and with Children) internationally. It is an academically focussed organisation that produces and supports a wealth of research and academic writings. In addition to their biennial conference, they also publish an academic journal, *Childhood and Philosophy*, and have an essay award competition, the winner of which gets published in the journal and invited to speak at the biennial conference. Quite uniquely, they invite all contributors to the journal to write in their mother tongue. More recently, ICPIC has had an increasing focus on bringing P4wC to more underprivileged children and teens.

To find out more head over to the ICPIC website: https://www.icpic.org/

Institute for the Advancement of Philosophy for Children (IAPC)

The IAPC is the birthplace of P4C. Matthew Lipman and Ann Margaret Sharp, the creators of Philosophy for Children, established the Institute for the Advancement of Philosophy for Children (IAPC) at Montclair State University in 1974.

Between 1974 and 1989 Montclair University piloted a wealth of research projects and implementation of P4C across America, but primarily in New Jersey. In 1990 the BBC produced *Socrates for Six-Year-Olds*, a one hour film on Philosophy for Children, which was broadcast in Britain, the United States, Japan, Israel, and other countries around the world. Interest in P4C mounted.

The IAPC now holds summer seminars, supports affiliate centres around the world. From 1979 to 2004 the IAPC published *Thinking: The Journal of Philosophy for Children. In 2002* Matthew Lipman retired from Montclair State University as Professor Emeritus; Professor Maughn Gregory becomes IAPC Director.

To learn more about the IAPC, head over to https://www.montclair.edu/iapc/

P4C China

P4C China is an internationally accredited training organisation offering in-school and public P4C (Philosophy for Children and Colleges) training to international and government schools across Greater China. They are based in Shanghai and deliver P4C training in Mandarin and English.

P4C China is a DialogueWorks International Partner who offers 3-4 year progression structured programs for schools wanting to embed P4C into their practice, values, and ethos. P4C China is a DialogueWorks accredited training centre providing P4C training for the Greater China region. To join the program, schools must intend to embed P4C in the teaching and learning in school, include P4C in the school's strategic plan, have school values which are consistent with those of P4C, commit to their teachers attending all of the training sessions, and commit to working with other P4C schools. On completion of the program, the school can then become a P4C Model School and be able to have continuous access to P4C china resources and support.

Cindy Zheng is the headteacher of Jintaiyang Fortune Kindergarten in Shanghai. She has been a P4C trainer since 2016. She is co-director of P4C China and regularly gives P4C training courses in Mandarin in government and international schools in China. Cindy is accredited as a DialogueWorks advanced level trainer.

See more about P4C China at http://www.p4c.org.cn/cn/index.aspx

P4C.com

P4C.com is a webs subscription service for teachers who would like to take a philosophical and P4C based approach to teaching. They provide resources, lesson plans, advice, collaboration, and tools for teachers to create their own materials. They are a registered co-operative and subscriptions enable the site to be maintained and developed, for editorial services to be paid for and for writers to be rewarded for their efforts.

When someone has contributed a certain number of resources, they have the option to apply for co-operative membership. Individuals and organisations can become members. They aim to raise awareness about the origins and ongoing development of Philosophy for Children (P4C). P4C.com contributes a 10% share of net subscription income to charities and projects that themselves promote philosophical inquiry. The Co-operative members of P4C.com are Steve Williams (Editor), Roger Sutcliffe, Kay Williams, James Nottingham, Grace Lockrobin, and Jason Buckley.

More information can be found at https://p4c.com/

SAPERE

Founded in 1992, SAPERE (Society for the Advancement of Philosophical Enquiry and Reflection in Education) is the UK's national charity supporting Philosophy for Children. SAPERE trains around 5,000 teachers, trainee teachers, and other educators each year. In addition to resources, conferences, seminars, and research projects, SAPERE also work with many universities to include P4C in initial teacher training courses.

They offer a Going for Gold programme to schools who would like to work towards whole school usage of P4C and accreditation.

Going for Gold schools work with their dedicated trainer over three years who collaborates with them to create a programme of training and support specific to their school ethos and needs. Schools then work through our Bronze, Silver, and Gold Awards and ensuring that your school reaps the benefits of a long-term commitment to P4C. The Going for Gold programme is open to all schools at primary and secondary levels.

https://www.sapere.org.uk/home.aspx

Sara Stanley

For anyone who does P4C in an Early Years setting, Sara Stanley will be a familiar name and, in particular, her books *Why Think?* And *But Why?* Sara Stanley is a National and International keynote speaker and runs workshops, Insets and courses in Philosophy for Children (P4C) and enabling enquiry based classroom environments.

Sara Stanley develops philosophical skills to enable children from as young as 3 to become critical thinkers and facilitators of ordered and structured dialogue, storytelling, and role-play. She offers a range of training opportunities and publications and is a registered level one SAPERE Trainer and half of the successful Children Thinking Consultancy with Maria Cornish based in Norwich Norfolk.

Sara Stanley has created a year-long story curriculum in which she entices the children to create their journey through one story, many books and dialogues, and enquiries based on their everyday play, language, and storytelling.

To learn more about the work of Sara you can find her website here: http://sarastanley.co.uk/?LMCL=lod05f

SOPHIA

Emma Worley (of The Philosophy Foundation) is the current President of SOPHIA. The Sophia Network is the European Foundation for the Advancement of Doing Philosophy with Children. It aims to bring together different practices across Europe to help teachers and practitioners to learn and develop from and with one another.

SOPHIA holds annual Meetings for SOPHIA Network members for professional development, networking with other European P4C practitioners, sharing experiences, research and ideas, and for joint collaboration in Philosophy with Children projects.

http://www.sophianetwork.eu/

The Philosophy Foundation

Co-founded by Peter Worley and Emma Worley in 2007, The Philosophy Foundation is a registered charity that recruits, trains and accredits philosophy graduates and undergraduates to be able to facilitate philosophical enquiries with groups of children, teenagers, and adults. The Foundation also provides teacher training and resources. Outside of working directly with schools, The Philosophy Foundation promotes the use of philosophical enquiry within a variety of public sphere platforms such as workplaces, politics, and prisons. The Foundation currently conducts philosophical enquiries in 40 schools in and around London.

To learn more about Peter and Emma or The Philosophy Foundation then you can find their website here https://www.philosophy-foundation.org/executive-officers

The Philosophy Man

For those of you who are most observant, you may have already spotted the names 'Jason Buckley' and 'Tom Bigglestone' as the philosophers who worked with Roger Sutcliffe on his Thinking Moves book. The Philosophy Man was founded in 2008 and is now the UK's leading independent provider of P4C training and workshops. Jason and Tom send free P4C resources to over 17,000 educators worldwide, and train upwards of 2,000 teachers a year through INSETS and Keynotes in our streamlined and accessible Philosophy Circles approach to P4C.

Jason Buckley is the Founder and Director of The Philosophy Man. A former teacher, Jason is now an internationally renowned trainer, writer, and speaker on P4C, classroom dialogue, and stretching the more-able. Tom Bigglestone works with classes through his role at the Economist Educational Foundation, alongside his training role at The Philosophy Man. He has been Head of Department at both primary and secondary levels and in both the maintained and private sector. He has specialised for several years in P4C, and in 2014 was awarded The Walter Hines

Page scholarship, for which he spent time in the United States researching assessment of philosophical skills.

To learn more about The Philosophy Man you can find the website here: https://www.thephilosophyman.com/

Author and Contributor Biographies

Dulcinea Norton-Morris

Dulcinea is an Early Years teacher and writer from Lancashire, UK. With Qualified Teacher Status and Early Years Professional Status and as one of the nurseries involved in the pilot project "Hanen LLC, Learning Language and Loving It" (Education Endowment Fund). She specialises in child development and education from birth to five years. After gaining her law degree and working in the civil service for ten years she decided to do a second degree in English and retrain as a teacher. Since then she has worked in the preschool class of St Leonard's Primary School in Padiham and has done freelance writing and editing and became an Associate of DialogueWorks where she is proud to be one of the members of the Early Years international working group for Thinking Moves. Dulcinea's fiction work has been published with Bridge House LLC, Wyvern Press, and Knowonder. Her teaching resources can be found on TES Online (@MagicalEYFS) and her Thinking Moves resources can be found on the DialogueWorks website. Dulcinea also has a blog called *Magical Mess of the EYFS* and a *Magical Mess of the EYFS* Facebook Page (@MagicalEYFS). In 2020 she also became the Early Years advisor for toy company Playbalu.

https://magicalmess.weebly.com/

Amanda Hubball

Amanda Hubball has been an Early Years teacher, member of the SMT, and school governor for almost 25 years. Her uncompromising vision rests on three key concepts:- aspiration, inspiration, celebration. She believes that "Aspire high, inspire all and celebrate everything" fully encapsulates a creative and cutting edge curriculum that provides what she believes is every child's educational right. Human connections, be they physical, mental, spiritual, moral... .all serve as the foundations on which she believes a learning environment with purpose and impact is built upon.

Amanda has responsibility for many aspects of school provision, as Alfreton Nursery School where she dedicates her time and love, in a small school serving a close-knit community. P4C and metacognition are a huge part of the embedded creativity in the school and she coordinates this work across the indoor and outdoor curriculum. As a Specialist Leader of Education for the Alfreton Nursery Teaching School, she influences future teachers across all phases of education as well as inspire practicing professionals. Cognitive challenge threads through her leadership in school and empowers both children and adults alike to reach for the light ahead, enabling them to hear their own voice and pursue their own dreams.

Dr. Fufy Demissie

Dr. Fufy Demissie is Senior Lecturer in primary and early years at Sheffield Hallam University and a registered P4C trainer for SAPERE and DialogueWorks (Thinking Moves). She began her career as an early years teacher before starting a career as a teacher educator. She has successfully integrated P4C in the teacher education course at Sheffield Hallam University and has written book chapters and articles on P4C and young children's thinking development as well as teacher development in initial teacher education. Since 2016, she has trained PGCE and undergraduate students at Sheffield Hallam and York St John University in the principles and practice of P4C. She is currently a project lead for a SHINE funded project on using P4C-based thinking games to improve young children's engagement with traditional stories

f.a.demissie@shu.ac.uk

Ella Parker

Ella Parker is a 13-year-old student currently attending Ulverston Victoria High School (UVHS) in Cumbria. She has passions for writing and drawing manga and hopes to become an author and illustrator in the future. She also spends some of her time playing the piano and clarinet.

Gina Parker Mullarkey

Gina Parker Mullarkey is a freelance practitioner and trainer based in the South Lakes. Through her company 'Little Chatters' she delivers training on Global and Outdoor Education with a strong focus on Philosophy for Children. She is a registered trainer for Learning through Landscapes, DialogueWorks and the Society for Advancing Philosophical Enquiry and Reflection in Education (SAPERE). She likes asking questions, drinking tea and running!

https://www.littlechatters.co.uk/

Sorcha Corwin

Braddan Primary School, Isle of Man

Sorcha has worked in education since 2000 and she has extensive experience in working with children aged 0-11. She has practiced P4C for many years with children aged 3-11 and is now a Thinking Moves trainer in the Isle of Man where she works as a teacher. Her interest and passion for philosophy was first sparked when she was studying for her BA in Fine Art in Ireland. Sorcha has taught every year group across the primary age range and she is always always willing to reflect on her teaching, consider the value and implications of constructive feedback, trial new initiatives in education and has extensive experience in coaching and supporting colleagues when leading and managing change.

Jorge Sánchez-Manjavacas Mellado

Jorge Sánchez-Manjavacas Mellado (Ciudad Real, 1987) is a secondary school teacher. He started to use a *Café* philosophique or FiloCafé in differents places (Libraries, Educative informal spaces, etc.). Then, when he started to teach class in different grades and levels he discovered P4C and since 2015 he is working with the P4C program and others like "Wonder Ponder" and now "Thinking Moves". Now, Jorge is working with a Spanish team to translate the book "Thinking Moves" into Spanish.

www.koinefilosofica.org

Reviews

I know you are all busy, you are reading a book about the under-fives so I KNOW how busy you are. I feel your pain! If you enjoyed this book, however, please do hop over to Amazon and leave a review. Then you can finish that cold cup of tea or coffee that you forgot you had made (or treat yourself to a hot one!)

Wishing you all health, happiness, excitement, and tranquility in your Magical Mess of the EYFS.

Dulcinea

X

Further Reading

If this book has whetted your appetite for exploring more about philosophical teaching then here are some suggestions for further reading. We, of course, will break the alphabetical flow, by starting with Thinking Moves.

Roger Sutcliffe with Tom Bigglestone and Jason Buckley, *Thinking Moves A-Z*, DialogueWorks (2019)

Jason Buckley, Pocket P4C, One Slice Books; 3rd edition (17 Jan. 2012)

Dr. Seuss and Philosophy: Oh, the Thinks You Can Think! (Rowman & Littlefield Publishers, 17 Jun. 2011) Jacob M. Held

Philosophy for Children Through the Secondary Curriculum (Continuum Publishing Corporation, 19 July 2012) Nick Chandley

Jostein Gaardner, *Sophie's World*, Phoenix (1995)

Berys Gaut (Author), Morag Gaut (Contributor), *Philosophy for Young Children*, Routledge; 1 edition (17 Aug. 2011)

Alison Gopnik, *The Philosophical Baby: What Children's Minds Tell Us About Truth, Love and the Meaning of Life: What Children's Minds Tell Us about Truth, Love & the Meaning of Life,* Bodley Head; Reprint edition (6 Aug. 2009)

Charles Furneyhough, *The Baby In The Mirror: A Child's World From Birth To Three,* Granta Books (6 April 2009)

Dominic Smith, *The Bird and the Elephant: Philosophy for Young Minds,* Joseph & Simon Publishing (1 Aug. 2017)

Fern Sussman, *More Than Words*, Hanen Centre; 2nd ed. edition (15 Mar. 2012)

Peter Worley, *40 Lessons to Get Children Thinking: Philosophical Thought Adventures Across the Curriculum*, Bloomsbury Education (22 Oct. 2015)

Peter Worley, *The Philosophy Foundation: The Philosophy Shop (Paperback): Ideas, Activities and Questions to Get People, Young and Old, Thinking Philosophically,* Independent Thinking Press (30 Jun. 2016)

Journals

Demissie, A., & Doxey, C. (2020). Trainee teachers' explorations and reflections on using picture books and the P4C (Philosophy for Children) pedagogy during story time. Literacy 4-11. *Literacy 4-11.*

Demissie, F. (2020). The Philosophy for Children pedagogy in a university-based initial teacher training course: a case study of a 'disruptive' pedagogy. *Forum for Promoting 3-19 Comprehensive Education, 62* (1), 69-78. http://doi.org/10.15730/forum.2020.62.1.69

Internet Publications

Demissie, F.A. (2019). P4C: a dialogic pedagogy for creative conversations. https://mon.uvic.cat/grell/philosophy-for-children-p4c-a-dialogic-pedagogy-for-creative-conversations/

Printed in Great Britain
by Amazon